Speed
Learning
for Kids

Speed Learning for Kids

The Must-Have Brain-Training Tools to Succeed at School

BILL HANDLEY

Wrightbooks

First published in 2013 by Wrightbooks
an imprint of John Wiley & Sons Australia, Ltd
42 McDougall St, Milton Qld 4064

Office also in Melbourne

Typeset in Trump Mediaevel-Roman, 11pt

© Learning Unlimited Australia Pty Ltd 2013

The moral rights of the author have been asserted

National Library of Australia Cataloguing-in-Publication data:

Author:	Handley, Bill.
Title:	Speed learning for kids: the must-have brain-training tools to succeed at school/Bill Handley.
ISBN:	9780730377191 (pbk.)
Notes:	Includes index.
Subjects:	Learning.
	Effective teaching.
	Educational innovations.
	Educational change.
	Dewey Number: 371.102

Cover design by C. Wallace

Cover image: © iStockphoto.com/Nicole S. Young

Internal design: Peter Reardon, pipelinedesign.com.au

Silhouettes: allsilhouettes.com

Examples in chapter 6 adapted from *Brain Stretchers* by Eugene Raudsepp

Printed in China by Printplus Limited

10 9 8 7 6 5 4 3 2 1

Disclaimer

# Contents

Acknowledgements

I owe so much to so many for the existence of this book.

First, Geoff Wright, founder of Wrightbooks, who phoned me after a radio interview and said, 'Write a book and I will publish it.' He was prepared to take a risk and it paid off. Thank you Geoff.

Thank you also to Geoff's daughter, Lesley Beaumont, who gave me heaps of guidance, advice and encouragement with my earlier books.

Thank you to the educators around the world and to the lecturers at teachers college who have encouraged me and helped me along the way.

I would like to thank the people at Wiley directly connected with this book. I would like to thank Lucy Raymond, Meryl Potter, Elizabeth Whiley and Keira de Hoog. They have all played an important part in the preparation of this book. There are so many others at Wiley who deserve thanks. I am grateful for your support.

I would like to dedicate this book to my grandchildren and to students everywhere.

Introduction

When I was about six or seven years old, my father took a special training course related to his work. His method of consolidating what he had learned was to come home and teach me his summary of the training program for that day. Although I was very young, I still understood most of what he told me. (Or I thought I did.) One evening he came home and told me that, instead of the regular training program, they had a special lecture on how to learn effectively. He explained how you have to link the new information to information you already know. If the connection is strange, crazy or even a bit risqué, all the better. I never forgot this, and used the basic strategy all through school and college—especially for cramming before exams. When my father asked me where I got the idea for my study methods, I told him he had taught me when I was about six years old. He said he remembered the course and teaching me at night, but he couldn't remember anything about the lecture on study methods (or even doing it), and he told me he had never used any of the methods himself.

In 1979 I developed my methods further and couldn't believe the results. I was so excited I had to tell someone. I told a friend who was also studying, and he became excited and asked if I would teach a group of his friends. They were able to start using the methods immediately. I was encouraged by my lecturers at teachers college to further improve my methods and to see how they worked in the classroom.

I conducted special classes for gifted students as well as students who were considered unteachable at the secondary school where I was teaching. After two months it was impossible to tell which class was which. This was reported in a local newspaper and resulted in a mother writing to me from New Zealand, asking if I could help her nine-year-old daughter who was terrified of maths. I recorded a cassette lesson and typed some notes and mailed them to her. She wrote back that her daughter had immediately played the tape and there was an immediate improvement in her maths. I made recordings of my other methods for study and literacy and had them professionally printed and packaged.

I received invitations to teach my methods to teachers and students around Australia, and then around the world, and I have continued to write about and teach them to this day.

How to learn effectively

During the first years of our life we learn at an incredible rate. We make our entry into the world knowing nothing—absolutely nothing. We don't know what or who we are or what anything else is. We find we can see and we can hear, but we have no idea what anything means—we can't make sense of anything. We soon learn to recognise people, sounds and our surroundings. We begin to make sense of it all.

Consider how quickly we learn our first language. We are able to get by and make our wishes known in a very short time. Then we learn how to express ourselves properly and speak about a variety of subjects.

Toddlers are desperate to learn and they are full of questions. They are always asking why, why, why? Their minds are like sponges, soaking up information.

School changes that. When we begin school we learn a whole lot of rules and our learning and our thinking become regimented. Teachers decide what we will learn, and when, and how we will learn it. Our questions can go unanswered if it doesn't suit the teacher's lesson plan. We are told to wait, and often we will never follow up our questions.

We are told what we have to learn but no one teaches us how to learn. We are left to work that out for ourselves. We are told to pay attention, try harder, concentrate. But nobody tells us how to do any of those things. How are we supposed to try harder? How do we concentrate on something we don't understand?

Children will punch the side of their heads to show they are trying, but it only succeeds in giving them a headache. They need someone to teach them *how* to learn. They would like to try harder, but nobody explains *how* to go about it. Too often they get discouraged and simply give up; they feel they lack the intelligence to learn in the way they are expected to.

Some students develop effective learning methods for themselves and seem to learn easily and well. They soon develop a reputation for being intelligent and fast learners. Others adopt very complicated and inefficient methods. Generally speaking, it is the methods we use that determine our learning ability rather than the quality of the brain we were born with. We can all greatly improve our ability to learn and to process information. This book will guide you through an effective learning process that will deliver unbelievable results.

Good students use better methods

One method of learning uses shortcuts and rhymes, and most of us have learned shortcuts or easy ways to remember information at school or at home. What are the seven colours of the rainbow? Red, orange, yellow, green, blue, indigo and violet. How can we remember the colours and remember them in order? If you can remember the name, Roy G. Biv, then you know the initial letters of the colours. R is red, O is orange and Y is yellow, and then we have Green, Blue, Indigo and Violet.

How many of us learned the rhyme, 'Thirty days hath September, April, June and November...'? That was an easy way to remember how many days there are in a month.

If you have studied music you will have learned easy ways to remember the notes of written music. 'Every good boy deserves fruit' or 'every good boy does fine' (EGBDF) will enable you to remember the lines of music, and FACE reminds you of the notes in the spaces between the lines.

Good students use better methods to learn, and good teachers use better methods to teach so students will learn. High-achieving students will look for easy ways to learn and remember what they are studying: they learn, for instance, to apply these kinds of shortcuts to other subjects they are learning. This means they are in control of the learning process. I call this active learning.

Ineffective and inefficient learning methods

The most effective method of learning is to make sense of the material you are studying. A lot of the information we have to learn simply makes sense. But, you still have to remember the points or arguments for the material that makes sense. Other information has to be learned by rote. This is stuff like dates, populations, distances and events that can't be reasoned.

The most common method of learning used by students the world over is to simply keep repeating the information they want to learn over and over until it sticks inside their brain. I call this passive learning, because the student is hoping that the information will stick by itself. This is rote learning. It is boring and you will tire of it quickly.

In this book, I am going to teach you an easy method of active learning, which puts you in control of the learning process. You will discover you can enjoy learning the most boring material, even subjects that you hate.

And, instead of repeating the material over and over, you will generally learn it the first time you take it in. Any repetition after this is just revision to ensure the information is in your permanent, or long-term, memory—available when you need it.

 Tips

- Better students use better learning methods.

- Nothing motivates like success.

- Children who learn these methods at an early age will use them for the rest of their lives.

- Students who see results for their efforts will put in even greater effort.

Who is this book for?

Children of any age (and their parents) can benefit from this book.

Example: Learning and wanting to learn

A family in Western Australia obtained an audio recording of my lessons to help their 11-year-old daughter. They played it while they were driving their campervan across the West Australian desert. The recordings began by giving 15 unrelated words and then told the listener to call back the 15 words in the correct order from memory. The girl did so. Then she was asked to call the words in reverse order and she did so without a mistake.

Then another voice was heard from the back seat. The three-year-old daughter asked if she could call out the words. She called them back without a mistake, both forwards and then backwards, much to her family's amazement.

You are never too young and never too old to learn the simple methods I teach in this book. And I promise I will make learning an enjoyable experience for you, whatever your age or past experience.

By the end of this book I guarantee you will perform like a genius.

Bill Handley
Melbourne, Australia
bhandley@speedmathematics.com
www.speedmathematics.com

Part I
The brain-training tools

In part I we will look at strategies that will enable you to learn what you read as you read it and what you hear as you hear it. You will learn to perform like a genius!

The difference between the top students and the bottom students is not so much the quality of their brain, but how they use it. You will learn strategies that will improve your performance out of sight. And the methods are fun to use and will make learning fun. The strategies are not complicated—they are easy to learn, and you can start using them immediately.

So, read the book, use the methods and perform like a genius. I wish you success.

Chapter 1
Making mental pictures

In 1982 a newspaper published an article about special classes I was conducting at the secondary school where I was teaching. They reported that students claimed that, using my methods, they could do the equivalent of more than two hours study in less than 10 minutes.

I was teaching two classes, one for gifted students and another for kids that other teachers considered unteachable. After a couple of months, both groups performed as if they were gifted. A group of students actually approached the school administration and complained that you had to be extra smart or extra dumb to get into my classes. This certainly took away any stigma of being part of the unteachables class.

I taught my system of mathematics, logical thinking, and learning and study techniques. I told the students that it is not the quality of your brain that determines your abilities, but how you use it. High achievers use better methods than the low achievers. I told them I would teach them better methods than the high achievers use so they will get better results.

Using your imagination to improve your learning is a good first step. Your imagination is a powerful tool for creating ideas, understanding ideas and learning ideas.

In this chapter we will see how you can harness your imagination to learn more effectively and efficiently. I'll use the example of showing you how you can use your imagination to learn the names of capital cities around the world.

Imagination and learning

Children are often told, 'Don't daydream!', 'Pay attention!', 'Concentrate!' This is *not* good advice, as the children who have a vivid imagination do best in school.

I daydreamed all my way through school and it helped immensely at examination time. As my geography or history teachers described what was happening in some far-off place or time, I would see it all in my mind. I ran it in my mind like a movie. Rather than hindering concentration, it enabled me to concentrate better and to understand better what I was hearing in class. And then, at examination time, I just re-ran the movie in my mind and got the answers I needed.

When I read a novel or a history book I always picture what I am reading. Most people do this. If I can't see what's happening, I have difficulty understanding it. That is why many people are disappointed when they see a movie version of a book: it's not how they pictured it in their minds.

If you can daydream, you can concentrate at a high level. This is great news for most kids.

Active learning is the secret

Most people never get beyond passive learning. They learn by rote: they learn by reading or listening to information over and over again, hoping the information will stick in their mind by itself and they will be able to recall at least some of it when they need it.

Better students look for ways to take control of the learning process. They continually ask themselves, how can I best remember this? What is the easiest way for me to learn it? They might think: that number is the same as the final digits of my friend's telephone number. Or that number is the same as our old street address, or the same as my sister's age.

Better students will look for the sense of what they are learning. They will ask themselves, why is it like that? Is there a reason, or what is the reason? If the thing can be reasoned, then they can use the same reasoning later in an exam to recall the information. The benefits go further if you actually use the information you have learned. Each time you use the information you are revising it.

Active learning takes place when you decide how you will remember what you are learning—you take charge of how you learn.

Have you ever had somebody explain something to you, and you told the person you understood what you had been told but, when you tried to explain it back to them, you couldn't do it? You thought you understood it but found out you didn't when you were tested. That is why many people say the best way to learn is to explain it or teach it to someone else. That is another example of active learning.

My speed learning method harnesses daydreaming and mental pictures and a system of reminders, which is a ready-made system of active learning. You decide how you will learn the information by making the mental pictures to connect what you want to learn with the reminders. By making sense of the information and by using the reminders (both are active learning strategies) you understand what you are learning and you can recall it under pressure.

Active learning is much more efficient and much more effective. You control the learning process, and you will see immediate results.

Joining new information to a reminder forces you to concentrate on what you are reading or hearing. It means you make the picture in your mind and that makes you concentrate at an even higher level.

Linking new information to old information

When my father recounted his training session on how to learn effectively he said you had to join the new information to information you already know. His advice has stayed with me all of my life. If you can make the connection using your imagination, then the learning process is even easier and better. This process is called linking information.

Let's see how this works by learning the names of some capital cities.

Learning the names of capital cities

Let's begin with the capitals of some South American countries.

Capital of Ecuador

If you know something about the city you could use a monument or landmark to represent the city, such as the Eiffel Tower for Paris, or Big Ben or the Tower Bridge for London.

Otherwise, I use a word that sounds like the country or city. For instance, Quito (pronounced KEEtoe) is the capital of Ecuador. We learn that the capital of Ecuador is Quito by finding a way of joining (or linking) the two names together. Here is where you use your imagination. Quito and Ecuador can be hard to join, so the next step is to look for words that sound like the names to make them easy to learn.

We ask ourselves, what do the names sound like? This forces us to concentrate on the names we are learning. You are not just passively reading or listening to the information; you are actively using it. I think that Quito sounds like mosquito so I use mosquito as my substitute word for Quito, and I see a mosquito. Ecuador sounds like equator (it actually means equator in Spanish) or 'aqua door'. When you use your imagination to join the two, you will remember them — even under pressure.

If I use equator as my substitute for Ecuador, I picture in my mind millions and millions of mosquitos swarming around the equator so no one wants to cross for fear of getting hundreds of mosquito bites. If I use aqua door as my substitute, I picture painting my door with aqua coloured paint, and mosquitoes land on the newly painted door and get stuck in the wet paint so I have to clean up the door and paint it again. Adding some action to the image can help make it stick in your mind.

Whichever picture you decide on, see it clearly in your mind and in as much detail as you can. This forces a high level of concentration because your mind can't drift elsewhere or you lose the picture. So, don't just agree with the pictures I suggest — actually see the pictures in your mind as clearly as you can. That is what forces high concentration and enables you to recall the information when you need it.

It's that simple — if you have seen the picture in your mind then you have memorised the name of the capital of Ecuador. It was easy and it was fun. And it required no more concentration than it takes to daydream.

Capital of Venezuela

Let's try another. Caracas is the capital of Venezuela. Caracas sounds like crackers and Venezuela sounds like…

What does Venezuela sound like? What do you do if you can't think of a word that sounds like the word you want to link? It doesn't have to be a perfect match. Whale sounds like the third syllable of Venezuela and it is the stressed or dominant syllable. That will work fine for me.

So, we need to link cracker to whale to remind us that Caracas is the capital of Venezuela. I picture a whale that has been beached and can't get back in the water. It is hungry so I give it some crackers to eat. Or, some naughty children have put firecrackers under the whale to try to shift it. Either picture makes the connection between crackers and the whale. Picture them both if you like and you have learnt the capital of Venezuela and have it memorised, ready for when you need it.

Capital of Peru

Lima is the capital of Peru. I think of lima beans for Lima and, if you imagine they have a bad smell and picture lima beans stink, pee-ew. That links Lima with Peru. Imagine holding your nose as you eat lima beans. See it happening in your mind. You won't forget it.

Capital of Romania

Let's take a European capital now: Bucharest is the capital of Romania. Bucharest sounds like book rest, and Romania sounds like remain here. We put bookends (rests) on our shelves so the books won't fall off—they 'remain here'.

Let's check what we have learned

Now, what is the capital of Ecuador?

What is the capital of Venezuela?

What is the capital of Peru?

What is the capital of Romania?

That was easy, wasn't it? Can you see that you can make learning subjects you find boring, or even hate, interesting and entertaining. If your mental pictures don't entertain you, whose fault is that? You can make learning any subject as entertaining as you want just by using your imagination and doing a little daydreaming.

Let's try this the other way around.

Of which country is Caracas the capital?

Which country has Lima as the capital?

Bucharest is the capital of which country?

Where is Quito?

You have learnt the information both ways. The city reminds you of the country and the country reminds you of the city. And we took the hard work out of learning it.

Here are some more to try

How would you remember that Budapest is the capital of Hungary?

Or that Santiago is the capital of Chile?

Or Helsinki is the capital of Finland?

Try to make your own connections before you read my suggestions.

It is easy to think of a word that sounds like Hungary (hungry) but what sounds like Budapest. The pest part of the word is easy, but what can we do with buda?

I imagine I am hungry and sit down to a meal, but a pest keeps interrupting my meal and I can't enjoy it. If I picture booing the pest each time he appears then I have my connection. I booed a pest because I am hungry and want to eat. So I'll remember, Budapest is the capital of Hungary.

Chile sounds like chilly. I picture Santa is trying to go down the chimney, but he gets stuck and gets cold because the weather is chilly. I join Santa with chilly for my connection.

I can find the words hell and sink from Helsinki and fin land from Finland. I picture being in the ocean and I see a shark fin circling me. That is enough to remind me of Finland. The shark from hell wants to sink me so it can eat me. That reminds me of Helsinki.

You will get better at making these connections with practice.

Making better mental pictures

If you make your mental pictures stronger and more memorable, you can force greater concentration on the information you want to remember and make it easier to recall when you need it. Here are some suggestions:

- Make the item bigger—make it *huge*.

- See millions of the object you are thinking of. Don't see just one mosquito—see millions stuck on your door.

- Make the items do something so you can see plenty of action: the mosquitoes are marching, hitting, biting, running and flying.

- Think of something being done to the objects you are seeing: they are being hit, squashed or eaten.

- Make the picture ridiculous—we forget the ordinary things in life but we remember the unusual. Making weird pictures in your mind forces you to think harder about what you are learning as you try to make them ridiculous. You are then less likely to forget the information. This will also help develop your ability to think creatively.

- See the picture as clearly and with as much detail as you can. And don't just see your picture—hear and feel it, if you can, rather than just see it.

- Try to involve your other senses in your mental picture to make it more real. Hear and feel your association, if you can, rather than just see it.

All of these rules will force you to concentrate, not only on the pictures but also on the information you are learning. You can use this method to learn anything: you are now in control of how you learn and the learning process is fun.

Practise making mental pictures to learn and remember information and you will not only learn more effectively and efficiently, but be able to recall information under pressure. You will also improve your concentration and develop other mental skills, and you will have fun while you do it.

Now let's see how well this has worked

Can you still remember, what is the capital of Finland?

The capital of Ecuador?

What is the capital of Hungary?

Venezuela?

Chile?

Peru?

Romania?

Do you see how well the method is working? You have just learnt and mastered a very useful learning tool.

 ## Tips for remembering

- Revise what you learn within five minutes of learning it.

- You only need to keep your first connections for five minutes.

- Do your second revision within an hour.

- Revise when you go to bed.

- Revise when you wake up.

After your first revision, just recite them once or twice a day for a week and afterwards, whenever you think of it. It is a painless and pleasant way to learn.

How long will I remember what I have learned?

People often ask me this question, but there is no easy answer.

If I am learning a list of things to buy from the supermarket this afternoon, then the information will stay until I have bought them. I don't need the information any longer so I only keep it in my memory for a couple of hours.

But what about studying for an exam? Tests and exams can be weeks or even months after we have learned the new information. The simple answer is that you need to put the information into your permanent memory so you can recall the information when you need it.

How to remember new information for a long time

After you have heard or read the new information you want to remember and joined each key point to one of your reminders, quickly review what you have learnt using the reminders. That is your first revision. You should do your first revision as soon as possible after you have memorised the list.

You should do your second revision no more than an hour later. Revise what you have learned while you walk to the bus stop, wait at the bus stop, travel home, wait in line at the supermarket checkout or while you walk your dog. If you have jobs to do after school, revise your schoolwork then.

When you put on your pyjamas to go to bed, run through the list again. They say you remember what you have learned better if you sleep immediately afterwards, so revise just before you go to sleep. And when you wake up in the morning, go through them again while you are thinking about getting up. Then go over the list once a week for a month and then from time to time when you think of it, and you will find the information will go into your permanent memory.

Revising what you have learnt while you are cleaning your room, mowing the lawn, or doing some other job that doesn't need your full attention means you aren't taking time from other activities to study. I call this using lost time to study. That means you aren't taking time from other activities to do your schoolwork. You would be doing those things anyway. In fact, it would appear to anyone else that you aren't doing any study but you are getting more accomplished than your friends who might be sitting up half the night.

Key points

- You can control how you learn.

- If you can daydream you can concentrate.

- Use your imagination to force high concentration.

- We remember the unusual more easily than the ordinary.

- We join new information to information we already know.

 Activities to try

- Try memorising the capital cities of other countries around the world, or the state or provincial capitals in the United States or Canada.

- Try memorising the captains and coaches of football or cricket teams. Have fun with the method.

Chapter 2
Using rhyming reminders

I have taught this method of learning around the world and for many years now. I encourage students to use the method in the classroom as well as showing off to their friends. They challenge their friends to call out words in random order and they call them back in the correct order. It seems impossible so the students often complain that no one will believe what they have actually done. Their friends and family tell them that no one can do that: it must be a trick, because you would have to be a genius to do that.

I tell my students never to argue with anyone who says you are a genius. I tell them to stand in front of a mirror and practise looking humble, and say, 'Oh, it was nothing', but if you tell them how you did it they will say it *was* a trick after all. Just let them think you have a fantastic brain.

The reminder system of memory training

The earliest system of memory training was called the place system. When a person prepared a speech, he would join the different points or topics of his talk with the different parts of his own home, or a place he knew very well. This served as a mental filing system. All the speaker had to do when giving the speech was take a mental walk through his home, using the places as reminders. The speakers might use the front gate to remind them of the first point, the front door to remind them of the second, the lounge room for the third, the back door for the fourth, and maybe the clothesline would remind them of the conclusion. This is believed to be the origin of the saying, 'in the first place, in the second place', and so on, and the word topic comes from the Greek word *topos*, which means place or location. The method is more than 2000 years old.

If you use a mental filing system, when you learn new information you can then file each piece of information in its proper place so you can get it when you need it. It uses a system of reminders.

Here is a list of reminders that you can easily learn in less than a minute—but instead of using places in your home as pegs for the new information, we will use rhyming words to help us memorise information as fast as we get it. We would all have different places for our reminders, but the rhyming list will work for anyone, no matter where they live. If you know the rhyme, 'one two, buckle my shoe', you already know half of the reminders. Here they are.

Rhyming reminders for numbers

1 run

2 shoe

3 tree

4 door

5 hive

6 sticks

7 heaven

8 gate

9 dine

10 hen.

The reminders are easy to remember because they rhyme with the number they represent. Say them out loud. One, run. Two, shoe. Three, tree. Now, to make sure you remember them, I want you to *see* each of them in your mind as you say them through again. Picture each reminder for about one or two seconds.

Now close the book and call them back from memory.

You found that easy, didn't you? Well, you reply, it was easy. I just had to learn rhyming words. I already knew half of them. But that's different from learning the stuff I have to learn every day.

The easy list you have just learned so easily will make learning the hard stuff just as easy. In fact, you will be amazed at what this system can actually do for you. The system makes sense, but the benefits seem to be out of proportion to what seem like reasonable results.

Here is how we use it, using the example of learning the characteristics of living things.

Learn the characteristics of living things

A grade five student told me he had to learn a list of characteristics of living things for his biology class. In other words, what are the things that tell you that something is alive? Here are the characteristics he had to learn. We learned them together in the order they were written in his textbook.

Number one—living things move. We join this idea to our reminder system, one, run. The connection we made is if you are running you are moving. In fact, you are moving twice over. You are moving from one place to another and you are moving your limbs and your whole body. Picture that and you have learned it.

Number two—living things eat and drink. Join this to our reminder for number two, shoe. I picture we go to the fridge for a drink of milk. We don't have a glass so we take off our shoe and fill it and drink from the shoe. That way we won't need flavouring. See yourself doing it! You can finish the picture by eating the shoe if you like. But your natural memory will fill in the extra details you need. You just need to be reminded of the second characteristic.

Number three—they reproduce (that means they have babies). Join that to three, tree. I picture the tree in my yard with lots of baby trees growing up around it. The seeds have fallen out and produced little baby trees. See it happening in your yard if you can.

Four, door—they react. I told the student to picture accidentally slamming the door to his room in his brother or sister's face and they react with their fist right in the student's face. Picture it for yourself.

Five, hive—they breathe. That is easy. Picture yourself standing next to a beehive and taking in huge breaths, huge lungfuls of air. With the air, you are breathing in bees from the hive. Now breathe them out. See it and you have already learned it.

Six, sticks—they are made of cells. Here I cheat a little. Instead of body cells I picture prison cells. And, instead of iron bars on the windows, what do they have? Sticks. Picture it and you have learned it.

Seven, heaven—they grow. When I was very young, maybe two or three years old, I remember noticing that the kids who were older than me were bigger. So, five year olds were bigger than two year olds, and nine or ten year olds were bigger still, and fifteen or sixteen year olds were even bigger again. I came to the conclusion that the older you were, the bigger you would be.

When I was little, I asked my parents, does anyone live to 100? (100 was probably the biggest number I knew.) My mum and dad said, yes, some people live to 100. I thought to myself, boy, they must be big. They must be huge. No one had ever explained that you stop growing in your teen years. I thought of living to be 100 and being able to step across rivers and having to duck my head when a plane flew over. I thought that would be great fun.

So, for seven, heaven, they grow, I thought of growing so big my head would actually be in the heavens among the clouds, and I pictured having to duck my head to dodge planes as they flew by. See that picture for yourself. Picture you have grown so big that your head is up above the clouds.

There, you have learned the seven characteristics of living things in record time with a minimum of effort. Call them back in the correct order, from one to seven.

Let's see if you can remember

What was number one? Run reminds you of...

Two, shoe, was...

What was three, tree?

Four, door, reminds you...

What was five, hive?

And six, sticks?

And finally, what was seven, heaven?

Did you get them all? If you missed one, see the picture again in your mind, add more detail if you can, then call them all back this time. Close the book while you do it.

How did you go this time?

Now surprise yourself by calling them out in reverse order, from seven back to one.

Did you do it?

What was number five?

What number was eat and drink?

You have learned the information inside out, backwards and forwards, and in and out of order. You have not only learned it, you have thoroughly learned it. And you had fun doing it. The method you used took the drudgery out of learning.

Not only have you learned the information, you can call it back under pressure. You could even call back the list with people shouting at you and insulting you. Certainly, the pressure of sitting an examination wouldn't worry you. This learning system is a great cure for examination nerves.

Did you notice that the suggestions I gave for each picture were a bit strange or weird or ridiculous—like drinking out of your shoe and then eating it? Ridiculous pictures always work better than logical connections. We remember the strange and unusual but we forget the ordinary things that happen. Are you more likely to remember a car parked under a tree or a car parked on top of a tree? You would say, 'I will never forget the time they put a car on top of the tree in our street. I wonder how they did it.' Make your pictures strange and weird if you can. This will make them memorable.

When you make your own connections and mental pictures you will find the method works even better than using my connections, and you are in control of the learning process. This is what I mean by active learning.

Six properties of magnets — another example

I was filling in for a teacher taking an engineering class and I had to teach the students the properties of a magnet. I thought it was an ideal opportunity to teach my mental filing system but I was nervous. I was worried the students might think it was juvenile and be insulted. I decided to try it anyway.

I told the students we were going to learn six properties of magnets and I had a method to make learning easy. I taught them the rhyming reminders. I tested the students and they had learned the reminders without effort.

Then I said we would use them to learn the properties of magnets.

One, run — we join the first property with one, run. The first property is that magnets have poles — a north pole and a south pole. I said I picture the south pole looking like a telegraph pole or a flagpole. It keeps running around and you never know where you will find it. The prime minister sends you down to the South Pole to stop it running because it is upsetting world navigation and all the compasses have been affected. Picture the pole running and you are chasing it.

Two, shoe — the second property of magnets is that poles that are not alike attract each other but like (or similar) poles repel each other. Two is shoe, so I picture that your shoes stink and they repel anyone who wants to come near you. When you take your shoes off at night you are forced to leave them outside because they repel. That will remind you of the second property. Picture it.

Three, tree—the lines of force make a complete circuit. They go from one pole to the other and through the magnet to leave again. If you put iron filings on a piece of cardboard and place a magnet beneath you will see that the filings form a pattern and show the lines of force. I simply picture a circle of trees in the schoolyard. They make a complete circle. See it now.

Four, door—lines of force cannot be crossed. Picture a line across the doorway to your room. No one is allowed to cross your doorway. You stop anyone who tries.

Five, hive—the lines of force are densest at the poles. The concept makes sense, but you need to be able to remember this for your exam. Picture giant beehives at the North and South Poles and the bees are buzzing around. There are bees everywhere but they are most dense at the poles because that is where the hives are. See it.

Six, sticks—a magnet that is allowed to hang freely will point to the North and South Poles. I picture hanging a magnetic stick by a thread and it points to the North and South Poles.

I then asked the students, 'Have you learned the properties? Let's try you out.'

They called back the six properties of magnets without effort. They couldn't wait for their regular teacher to return so they could show off their new skill. Instead of being insulted they pleaded with me to teach them something else using this method. They thought it was great.

Now check that you have learned the properties of magnets. Close the book and call them back. That was almost like learning without trying, wasn't it?

Now call back the characteristics of living things.

Are you impressed? Although you used the same list of reminders, you were still able to put the information in the correct list. That is because your intelligence can tell you what is a property of a magnet and what is a characteristic of living things.

You can use this method to learn anything and to make your study more fun and more interesting. You are in control of the learning process. This is not rote learning because you have absorbed the information through really having to concentrate on what you were learning. And the learning process was fun.

Use the reminders to remind yourself of things you need to do or things you have to buy from the shops. This is a fun way to practise. (I have also included another fun way to practise your new skill at the end of this chapter.)

Making your own pictures in your mind works better than using the ones I give you because you have to think about what you are trying to learn and to think about a good, weird mental picture. It will force an even higher level of concentration, and therefore better learning.

Improving your understanding

People say to me, it is one thing to just remember information, what about understanding it?

The rhyming reminder method will actually help you to understand better what you are learning.

First, you have to ask yourself, what is the first thing they are saying? What does it mean? You are analysing what a teacher or the textbook is saying. Then you have to summarise your analysis. You should be able to say in one or two sentences what the first point is. You take the meaning of what your teacher is saying and link it to number one, run. If you don't understand what they are saying you will have trouble making a connection. So, you get instant feedback on whether you understand what you are learning or not. The reminder method of study actually improves your learning strategies and certainly enables you to achieve more with less effort.

The method also improves your concentration, as your mind can't wander while you are deciding on the mental pictures you will make, and then while you are actually making them.

As well as being an effective way to learn, rhyming reminders and making mental images are fun.

A fun way to practise

Here is a fun way to practise what you have learned and show off your skills.

Ask your friends or family to write the numbers one to 10 vertically down the side of a piece of paper. Then ask them to call out any number from the list and call out an object, and write it down alongside the number. Tell them not to call out the numbers in order but to mix it up. They could start with number six, then two, or any number they like. While they are writing the item down alongside the number, you make a mental picture joining the item with the reminder for the number. The time they take to write the items down should give you enough time to make a picture in your mind. If they go too fast, simply ask them to wait until you are ready for the next one. You are giving the demonstration so you make the rules. Tell them to keep calling numbers and objects until all of the numbers have been called with the objects.

Tell them the objects should be something tangible like desk, window, grass, bird or school—nothing intangible like love, greed, lie or confusion. The objects should be something they can see or feel.

Although your friends called the numbers and objects in random order, you will now call them back in the correct order. When you have amazed your friends by calling out all the numbers and objects correctly, surprise them even further by calling the items out as fast as you can in reverse order.

Then ask them for random numbers from the list and you will call out the items; then have them call the items and you will give the numbers. You have learned the information inside out in record time. You will get a reputation for being a genius.

It is possible that, in the middle of the demonstration, you will panic and be tempted to go back to items previously called to make sure you haven't missed them. Don't do it. Just concentrate on the new items they call. Otherwise you might be thinking of the previous items instead of the current one. Just make sure you make clear mental pictures, or clear crazy mental pictures, and you will remember them all. Deciding on a crazy picture is only half of the process—you must make a clear picture in your mind for the strategy to work.

Let's try an example to see how it works.

Example: a fun way to practise

Number six is hurricane. I picture a hurricane with *sticks*, big sticks, flying through the air and doing damage. You are trying to dodge them as they fly by.

Number three is MP3 player. Picture a *tree* in the schoolyard or your backyard growing MP3 players instead of fruit, or you have hidden your MP3 player at the top of the tree.

Number eight is cup of coffee. I picture painting your *gate* with a cup of coffee. You are using it as a stain. Make sure you *see* it.

Number one is a dictionary. Picture your dictionary *run*ning down the road and you are chasing it because you need it for school.

Number nine is a lunch bag. You could picture putting your lunch in your lunch bag to *dine* on later, but I prefer to picture myself actually eating my lunch bag. Decide which picture you want to use. See the picture as clearly as you can.

Number two is an orange. Picture wearing oranges on your feet for *shoes*. They squelch as you walk.

Number five is a clock. I picture a giant clock outside a bee*hive* for the bees to tell when to come and go. They come and go at the right time each day. They need an accurate clock to tell the time.

Number ten is a computer. I picture a *hen* using my computer and typing on the keyboard. See it.

Number four is pillow. Picture having a giant pillow for your bedroom *door*. When you want to be alone you lock the pillow instead of the door.

Number seven is racing car. I picture a racing car flying above the clouds — in *heaven*. Or you are in a plane and look out the window and see a racing car flying alongside you.

Okay, you have just memorised 10 items in jumbled order. Now call them back.

What was number one? What was *run*ning?

What was number two? *Shoe* reminds you of?

What was number three? What was on the *tree*? Growing on the tree?

What is number four? Your *door* reminds you of?

What is number five? Bee*hive* reminds you of?

Six was? Where were the *sticks*?

Seven, *heaven*, reminds you?

Eight, *gate*, was?

Nine was? *Dine*. What were you eating?

Ten was? Where was the *hen*? What was it doing?

What was number three? What was number eight? What was number two?

What number was dictionary? What number was pillow?

Now you call the list out backwards. That was even easier, wasn't it? But still very impressive. In fact, your friends and family will think you are a genius.

You have learned the list thoroughly and you are able to call back the information, even under pressure. That is exciting. Not many people can do what you just did. And it was so easy. And the fact that you were given the list in random order makes the exercise seem harder, but really it made no difference, it is just more impressive.

If you get stuck on an item in a practice session like this, ask yourself questions about the reminder for the number. Where was it? What was it doing? What happened to it? That will usually remind you of the one you have forgotten. But what do you do if you are unable to recall one of the items? You have asked yourself the questions and you still can't remember it. First, you say, I am having trouble with number five. I will come back to it, and quickly call out the rest of the list. Then try again. If you still can't recall the item, simply ask what it was.

Your friends will tell you the answer, clock. You make the mental picture again, improving it if possible, and then say, 'That's right. I am sorry. To make up for my lapse, I will now call out the list backwards.' One thing is certain: you won't forget number five this time. Your embarrassment will make sure of that.

Then when you ask your friends to call out a number and you will tell them the item, and then tell them to call some of the items and you tell them the number, you demonstrate you have not only learned the list, but you have learned it thoroughly. Your friends won't believe it.

Whenever one of my students misses an item his friends usually say afterwards, he pretended to miss one. He obviously didn't forget because he called back the list backwards, then we called out numbers and he called the object and then we called the items and he gave the numbers. He had the list learned inside out. He only pretended.

Don't tell your friends how you did it. Let them think you are a genius. You really did learn the list that they gave you. If you tell them how you did it they will say it was just a trick. To me, a trick implies trickery, which means you didn't really do it; it just looked like you learned them. You didn't pretend to learn the list—you really did it.

Now for a word of caution: don't do this exercise twice in the same day or you might confuse the lists. There is a way you can do the demonstration twice or three times in the same day but you would use different reminder lists. But you can use the same list over and over to memorise information that is not random—for instance, to memorise a shopping list, a list of things to pick up on your way home, a list of characteristics of living things or properties of magnets. In these cases common sense will tell you which list the items belong to and what kind of information you are looking for.

Key points

- American writer Mark Twain used rhyming reminders to memorise his talks so he could speak without notes.

- Rhyming reminders are easy to learn and help us learn more difficult information.

- Reminders and mental pictures help us to learn and recall under pressure.

- Using reminders and mental pictures helps us to understand what we are learning.

- Using reminders and mental pictures keeps our mind focused on what we are learning

- You can use the same reminders over and over to learn new material.

More activities to try

- ☝ Use the reminder system to help you learn from library books or the internet.

- ☝ Try using it to learn how to train your dog or look after your budgerigar.

- ☝ Use the method to memorise the things you want to do after school.

- ☝ Try using it to remind yourself of questions you want to ask someone.

Chapter 3
Learning look-alike reminders

I had just demonstrated my ability to memorise a list of words to a group of friends, as we did in the previous chapter. They were clearly impressed. When some more friends joined us, the first group told them what I had just done. They insisted I repeat the performance. Normally I would say no, because if you use the same reminders in quick succession you will mess up. I wanted to impress my friends, so I decided to use a different reminder list. I used my emergency reminders. I was able to call out both lists of words they had given me without a mistake.

There can be situations where you have to learn two lists of items in quick succession and there is nothing about the information to tell you which list it belongs to. Or, you have just given a demonstration of your learning abilities and you are persuaded to repeat the performance to another group that has heard about your amazing feat. That is when you need to use your emergency reminder list.

Instead of rhyming words, I use objects that look like the numbers they represent for my emergency reminders. They also allow me to learn anything where there are 20 items to remember. You will also learn these with practically no effort. And remember to *see* each connection in your mind as you read it. Here is my list.

Look-alike reminders

Here are my look-alike reminders. I have included pictures of the first two—try out the rest for yourself: the ones you decide on will work best for you.

1 A pencil—because an upright pencil looks like a number one. See it.

2 A swan—because a 2 looks like a swan. Can you see it?

3 A McDonald's restaurant—because 3 looks like a big capital letter M tipped over or, if you tip a 3 over, it will look like the golden arches outside a McDonald's restaurant. Picture it.

4 A sailboat or yacht—because the top of the 4 looks like the sail.

5 A nose or a hook—I think about nose here—the top of the 5 looks like the peak of a cap over a cartoon-type nose.

6 A yoyo—can you see the yoyo at the bottom of the string?

7 A boomerang—because it looks like the Australian Aboriginal throwing device that returns to the thrower.

8 A robber's mask or the Lone Ranger's mask—another one where you have to tip the 8 on its side so it looks like two eyeholes.

9 A tape measure—I picture the retractable tape measures used by carpenters where you press the button and the tape runs back into the holder.

10 A bat and ball—can you see them?

Now, please call out the look-alike reminders from one to ten from memory.

Easy, wasn't it, because there was no rote memory involved. The shape of the number helps you recall the reminder.

Now, you can either use these as an alternative set of reminders for 1 to 10 or you can use them as reminders for numbers in the teens to bring your number of reminders to 20. So, pencil would be your reminder for 11, swan for 12 and bat and ball for 20.

Let's try them out

Remembering a shopping list

We'll use the emergency reminders to memorise things you need to buy at the supermarket. Your family has invited friends to a barbecue and you have been sent to the supermarket to get some food for the party.

You arrive at the supermarket on your bike, only to discover that you left your list at home. Luckily, you memorised the items as your parents wrote them down so you don't need your list.

Shopping list

Milk

Coffee

Apples

Bananas

Potatoes

Bread

Sausages

Tomato sauce

Lettuce

Onions.

How would you remember these items? Here are my suggestions.

1 You picture drinking milk through a hollow pencil, using it as a straw.

2 You see a swan swimming in a lake of coffee and the feathers turning brown.

3 You imagine yourself filling up on apple pies at a McDonald's restaurant. You eat a mountain of them.

4 You picture pirates boarding your yacht using bananas as guns.

5 You see yourself stuffing a big potato up your nose. Your nose turns into a potato!

6 See yourself playing with a giant yoyo using a round loaf of bread at the bottom of the string.

7 You are throwing curved sausages in the air and they come back to you like boomerangs.

8 You imagine robbers robbing the supermarket and squirting tomato sauce at anyone who disobeys them. 'Give me the money or I squirt!'

9 You see yourself measuring the lettuces in the supermarket with a tape measure because your family has told you they must be a minimum size.

10 You are using onions as balls and hitting them out of the stadium.

Make sure you see each link as clearly as you can in your mind.

Now close the book and call them all back from memory.

Did you get them all?

What was number 4? Yacht tells you...

What was number 8?

I use this strategy all the time. I mentally go over the reminders as I push my trolley through the aisles. I check that I have item one, two, three... I don't have number four and I head off to get it.

These methods don't just work for schoolwork—you can use them for anything you like.

Key points

- Use the look-alike or emergency reminders when you have two similar pieces of information to learn around the same time.

- Use the look-alike or emergency reminders for numbers in the teens, from 11 to 20.

- Remember to really *see* the picture you imagine — that makes the reminders work better.

- Try to make your connections funny or crazy or exaggerate — they'll be much easier to remember.

 More activities to try

- ☼ Try your memory stunt again on your friends, but this time ask them to give you 20 items to memorise. Use the rhyming reminders for one to 10 and the look-alikes for 11–20. You are improving your skills and becoming familiar with your reminders.

- ☼ Memorise the teams that won the premierships this season. Choose whichever sport you like.

- ☼ Memorise the names of your 20 favourite books or movies.

- ☼ Memorise 20 things you will have to buy friends and family for Christmas.

- ☼ Learn the names of the first 20 presidents of the United States given in chapter 15.

Chapter 4
Creating logical reminders

There may be times when you need to memorise more than 20 items or you need to perform your 10-item stunt more than twice. There are many ways to increase the number of reminders. You could use your family to help you remember stuff you need to know. You could use your parents for one and two, and then your brothers and sisters in order of age to make up the rest. If you are an only child you could use your cousins or friends to make up the numbers. You can also use the rooms of your house or maybe shops in a local shopping street that you know well, in the way the Greeks and Romans and public speakers used places to remind them of topics they needed to remember.

Increasing the reminders to 30

This list of reminders has a more logical connection with the numbers they represent. You can use this list for numbers in the twenties to bring your list of reminders up to 30, or you can use it as a third reminder list in an emergency situation. Here's my list.

The logical reminders

1 *One-way street*—I picture a narrow one-way street with the item to be remembered travelling the wrong way against the traffic. Choose a one-way street that you know if possible.

2 *Switch (on/off, two positions)*—I picture a big switch on the item and switching it off and on.

3 *Three blind mice*—simply join the mice to the information being memorised.

4 *Table (four legs)*—either see the item on your kitchen table or being used as a table.

5 *Hotel (five-star hotel, or a top-class hotel)*—think of a really flash hotel. You might like to picture the pool or a luxurious hotel room.

6 *Hitting a six in cricket*—is the equivalent to hitting a home run in baseball. See yourself hitting the ball over the fence and out of the stadium. Or you could use the sixth sense—telepathy or mind reading.

7 *7-Eleven store or 7Up drink*—picture a 7-Eleven store that you know.

8 *V8 super cars*—picture the item you have to remember in a race with V8 super cars or driving a V8.

9 *Cat, which is said to have nine lives*—picture a cat that you know—maybe your own cat.

10 *Hands or fingers*—we have 10 fingers so our hands are a natural reminder for 10.

If you can think of a better reminder for any of the numbers, then by all means use it.

Let's use my version to help us learn a list of Australian prime ministers in record time.

Tip

If you don't want to learn the names of the Australian prime ministers, look at chapter 15 to find out how to learn the names of the first 20 US presidents.

Learning the list of Australian prime ministers

We can use our 30 reminders to learn a list of the Australian prime ministers. You will find it is not difficult to learn them all at one sitting. Most students would not even dream of trying to do that, but learning the reminder methods has no doubt raised your expectations.

Up until now we have memorised concrete information — information that is easy to picture in your mind. But how do we memorise people's names? It is difficult to memorise a Fraser or Gorton or Howard. If the name has meaning we use the meaning itself, like Butcher, Baker or Curry.

With names like Fraser or Barton we ask ourselves, what does the name sound like? I think that Fraser sounds like freezer, which is much easier to picture. Barton sounds like bar ton, or a bar weighing a tonne. This is how we will memorise the names of the Australian prime ministers. The substitutes don't have to sound exactly like the names — they only have to sound enough like the name to remind us. If we are learning the list in class or for a real purpose, then that is all we need.

1 Barton
2 Deakin
3 Watson
4 Reid
5 Fisher
6 Cook
7 Hughes
8 Bruce
9 Scullin
10 Lyons
11 Page
12 Menzies
13 Fadden
14 Curtin
15 Forde
16 Chifley
17 Holt
18 McEwan
19 Gorton
20 McMahon
21 Whitlam
22 Fraser
23 Hawke
24 Keating

25 Howard

26 Rudd

27 Gillard.

Let's quickly learn them all. Make sure you see the connections clearly in your mind.

Let's learn 1 to 10

To learn the first 10, we use the mental pictures and rhyming reminders we have already learned in chapters 1 and 2.

1 *Run*—Barton. Imagine *run*ning but carrying an iron *bar weighing a tonne*, which slows you down.

2 *Shoe*—Deakin. Picture a *deacon* taking up the collection in church and collecting the money in a giant *shoe* instead of a plate.

3 *Tree*—Watson. Your *tree* is hard of hearing and it keeps saying to the baby tree, *What, son? What, son?*

4 *Door*—Reid. You have a list of rules written on your *door* for visitors to *read*.

5 *Hive*—Fisher. I picture using *bees* as bait to catch *fish*.

6 *Sticks*—Cook. *Cook*ing bird's nest soup (with *sticks*) over a fire or using sticks as fuel for the fire to cook.

7 *Heaven*—Hughes. Hughes sounds like huge. You are so *huge* you can see right up to *heaven*.

8 *Gate*—Bruce. Bruce sounds like bruise. Your front *gate* swings and hits you every time you use it, so you are covered in *bruises*. See it.

9 *Dine*—Scullin. Picture *sculling* down the river as fast as you can, while you *dine*, eating food for strength as you go.

10 *Hen*—Lyons. *Lions* at the zoo munch on *hens* for lunch.

Test yourself

Now call back the Australian prime ministers from one to 10.

That was easy. Now let's learn some more.

Let's learn 11 to 20

To learn prime ministers from 11 to 20, we again use the look-alikes we learned in chapter 3.

1 *Pencil*—Page. Picture turning the *page* of a newspaper with a *pencil*.

2 *Swan*—Menzies. Menzies sounds like men's. You can picture a whole line of *swans* waiting to use the *men's* room.

3 *McDonald's*—Fadden. Fadden sounds like fatten. You are eating up big at *McDonald's* to *fatten* yourself up.

4 *Yacht*—Curtin. You have a new yacht, and your mother makes new *curtains* to hang over the portholes.

5 *Nose*—Forde. Your *Ford* car has a huge *nose* in place of a radiator or your new Ford hits you on the nose and you get a nose bleed.

6 *Yoyo*—Chifley. Your *chief* (boss) uses a *yoyo* to hit the company staff on the head to keep them in line.

7 *Boomerang*—Holt. You train your *boomerang* to stop in mid flight when you call, '*Halt*'.

8 *Robber's mask*—McEwan. I had difficulty finding a sound-alike for McEwan. I thought of 'mock you', 'make you' or even 'sand dune'. In the end I decided the prime minister is trying to *make you* a *robber*. He is teaching you how to rob people effectively. Or a robber is hiding behind sand dunes at the beach to steal the swimmers' clothes.

9 *Tape measure*—Gorton. I am not sure what to use as my substitute for Gorton—tonne of gore? Or 'caught on' so I use both in the same picture. Your tape measure gets *caught on* the container when you are measuring a *tonne of gore*.

10 *Bat and ball*—McMahon. You cause *mayhem* when you are scoring 100 in cricket or a home run in baseball.

Test yourself

Now close the book and call out the prime ministers from one to 20. Did you get them all? If you missed one, make the picture again, add some detail (make it crazy if it will help you remember) and see it as clearly as you can. Then call the names out again without a mistake.

Let's learn 21 to 27

To learn the names of the prime ministers from 21 to 27 we use our new system of logical reminders.

1 *One-way street*—Whitlam. People are chasing a *white lamb* running the wrong way down a *one-way street*. Picture the white lamb and the cars dodging each other.

2 *Switch*—Fraser. The switch on your *freezer* is broken and the food spoils. See the broken *switch* and the food spoiling.

3 *Three blind mice*—Hawke. A *hawk* sees *three blind mice* and finds them an easy catch for lunch. See the hawk swooping down.

4 *Twenty-four, table*—Keating. If you remove the K from Keating you have eating, and that makes an easy picture of your family *eating* at the dining *table* or, even better, eating the table itself.

5 *Five-star hotel*—Howard. I ask myself, 'How hard (Howard) is it to build or to buy a *hotel*?

6 *Hitting a six*—Rudd. You hit a six using a ship's rudder instead of a bat.

7 *A 7-Eleven*—Gillard. Gillard sounds like kill yard. I picture *killing* chickens in the *yard* and selling them to *7-Eleven* stores.

You will join the 28th prime minister to V8 cars, maybe driving or getting hit by one, and you will join the 29th prime minister to cat.

With this method, you can memorise the Australian prime ministers in around 15 or 20 minutes. You could probably manage in less than 10, but it isn't a race.

And, you are probably the only person in your school who can call out all of the Australian prime ministers off by heart. That was the fastest and easiest way to learn them.

Learning abstract information

The general rule for learning abstract information when you don't know what it looks like or it is too vague to picture is to look for a word that sounds like the word you are trying to learn or look for something to represent the quality or the meaning.

And remember, using your own sound-alikes and pictures will work better than the ones you have been given. Making your own pictures will force a much higher level of concentration.

Tip

When you don't know what the word you are learning looks like or it is too vague to picture, look for a sound-alike word or for something to represent the quality or the meaning of the word you are learning.

Sound-alike or rhyming?

People have often asked me, why not just choose a word that rhymes with the word or name I need to remember? That would be easier.

When I choose a sound-alike I make the substitute word as close as I can to the word it replaces. If I change a consonant it is usually the phonetic equivalent. That is, I replace T with a D or B with a P. I might replace Ch with Sh, and F might replace V. The words will sound similar.

The problem with rhyming words is there can be too many names that rhyme with your substitute. You might choose a word that rhymes with John and then find you can't remember if the name was John, Don, Con, Lon or Ron. A word that rhymes with Jim might remind you of Jim, Kim or Tim. I think using sound-alikes is a much better and safer way to go.

Key points

- Use the logical reminders for numbers from 21 to 30.

- Use the logical reminders if you have a number of similar lists to learn.

- Look for a sound-alike word if the word you are learning is abstract or hard to visualise.

- If you can't find a sound-alike, find something to represent the word you are learning.

More activities to try

- You can use the reminders to memorise the jumper numbers of players on your football team.

- Try using the logical reminders to learn some lists of 10 items just for practise. You need to know the reminder lists well so you don't get stuck trying to think of the reminder when you need it.

- Memorise a list of presents you would like for Christmas.

Part II
Learn like a genius

In part II we will learn how to apply the methods we learnt in part I. You can apply these methods to every part of your life, not just for schoolwork. I use the system for play as well as for serious stuff.

Here is how I use my method for general learning. When I am listening to a talk I want to remember or I am reading something I need to learn, I am ready with my reminders before I begin. I am waiting for the first point and I am ready to join it to *run*. I make sure I see my picture in my mind as clearly as I can. This forces me to concentrate and helps me to listen or read with more interest than I might have normally. As I determine point number one, I see it running, chasing or being chased. Then I listen for the next point and I am ready with *shoe*. As soon as I hear there are four ways to, or six rules for, or five reasons why, or eight types of something, I am ready to use my reminders so I can learn them as I hear them. I do that automatically. I decide afterwards if I want to retain the information. That way I can memorise what I read as I read it and what I hear as I hear it.

Chapter 5
How to learn to spell like a genius

When I was a student at teachers college we were told that we should never correct a student's spelling mistakes. Not only would that inhibit creative thought, but who were we to say a student's spelling is wrong?

Unfortunately, this thinking is not shared in the workplace. I heard one boss say that if he got a job application with spelling errors he would throw it in the bin. And you don't want to make spelling mistakes if you are a sign writer, write advertising copy or if you are promoting educational material. A lawyer told me he would pay high wages to a secretary who could spell. Correct spelling is important if you are writing any kind of official letter, applying for a job or trying to sell a service.

Can we use our learning methods to remember correct spelling? Certainly.

Making links
We have already seen that one way of remembering new information is to join it to something we already know. To improve our spelling, we use an easy word to remind us of the correct spelling of a difficult word.

Some spelling rules

Here are some rules of spelling that can be applied to help us spell many words. Learning a few rules can help you spell many words correctly.

- If a word starts with a C it will be sounded as a K, unless the following letter is E, I or Y. Some examples of K sound for words spelt with a C are carry, can, close, cold, catch and cringe.

- When the letter following the K sound is E, I or Y, then the word must be spelled with a K. Some examples of K sound spelt with a K are keg, kiss, kill, ketch, kip and kerosene.

- If a C is followed by E, I or Y, the sound of the C changes to S. Some examples of E, I and Y changing the C to an S sound are centre, cereal, cellar, cinder, circus and cycle.

- A K sound at the end of a word is generally spelled with a K, such as week, cook, lark, bank and bark.

- A K sound at the end of a word is spelt with a CK if it follows a short vowel. Examples are back, hack, shack, neck, deck, shock, sock, luck and duck. (The long vowels are take, feet, like, hope and cute.)

- The letters E, I and Y can also change the sound of a G to a J sound when they follow it. Think of gender, giraffe, gem and gymnasium.

- A short O sound (like hop, spot, stop or shop) after a W is spelled with an A, like want, swap, wash, watch, wander, swamp, swallow, wallet, waffle and was. The word 'was' is pronounced as it is written! The rule tells you that 'was' should be spelled with an A.

Learning one or two rules can help you spell a multitude of words correctly.

What to do when you don't know the rule

What do you do if you don't know the rule or if the word is one of the exceptions to the rule? It is the exceptions that cause the trouble.

Here is how I remember the correct spelling of words that I have problems remembering.

Never believe a lie

When I was young, teachers taught us, never believe a lie. If we can spell the word 'lie' then we can remember the spelling of 'believe', because the word 'lie' can be found in the word be*lie*ve. In other words, we can use a word we do know to help us remember the spelling of a word we don't know.

A piece of pie

Another spelling trick they taught us was 'a *pie*ce of *pie*'. That taught us that piece, meaning a part of something, is spelt 'piece' and not 'peace'. It also helped us remember that 'i' comes before 'e' in this word.

We were taught the rule that I comes before E except after C. This rule applies when there is an 'ee' sound like chief, achieve, believe, and E before I after C, as in receive, deceit and ceiling.

Built on stilts

When I was in primary school I had difficulty remembering how to spell 'built'. I couldn't remember whether it was biult or built. But if I picture a house bu*il*t on st*il*ts I could remember the correct spelling. We join the word we know to the word we don't know. The spelling of stilts is easy and gives us the sequence ILT. That tells me the same combination occurs in built so I know it must be U followed by an I, which also tells me the correct spelling for 'build'.

Stationery or stationary?

How about the words stationery and stationary? Which word should be used when? You buy station*ery* from a station*er*'s. Or letters are stationery. When I sat for my driving licence test I learnt about station*ary* c*ars*. That should help you remember which spelling to use.

Here or hear?

I teach children that you h*ear* with your *ear*.

W*here* is it? It is *here*. Or it is t*here*.

And that helps you remember that you w*ear* earrings on your *ear*.

That sorts out here, hear, where, there and wear.

ible or able?

I remember having to write the word 'responsible'. I wasn't sure if it ended with 'able' or 'ible'. I checked in the dictionary, and then imagined, *I* am respons*i*ble for everything that goes wrong around here. I get the blame. That burned the correct spelling into my brain.

ar or er?

How do we remember that gramm*ar* and calend*ar* both end in *ar* and not *er*?

My grand*ma* will remind me of gram*mar* and it is a good idea to have a cal*enda*r when you are writing an ag*enda*.

Delagate or delegate?

Do you spell the word delagate or delegate? I picture you de*leg*ate someone to do all of the *leg* work for you.

Complement and compliment?

People often confuse the words complement and compliment. Here's my method for remembering the correct spelling.

I like to be complimented reminds me that the expression of praise is spelt with an I. If *I* imagine that people comp*lim*ent me on my ability to c*lim*b mountains, it will remind me of the spelling.

Anything that *comple*ments something can also be said to *complet*e it.

Seperate or separate?

Is the correct spelling seperate or separate? I picture that we all travel in sep*ar*ate c*ar*s. That is enough to remind me of the correct spelling.

Working out your own reminders

It is not hard to come up with your own reminders for words you are not sure of. Every time you check the spelling of a word in a dictionary or using your computer's spell-check, commit the correct spelling to memory. Just find the part of the spelling you are not sure of, find a word you already know how to spell that has the same spelling somewhere in it, and then make a mental picture that joins the two.

Alphabet reminders

You can also use these handy alphabet reminders to help you remember how to spell words that look tricky. They can be useful if you can't think of another word with the same letter combination that you need. The alphabet reminders can also be useful for memorising lists or part numbers or car number plates comprised of both letters and digits. They can also be used as an alternative set of reminders in an emergency.

My alphabet reminders

a   ape/hay

b   bean

c   sea

d   dean

e   eel

f   ref (referee)

g   gee-gee (horse)

h   ache

i   eye

j   chase

k   key

l   hell

m   ham

n   hen

o   eau (French for water as in eau de cologne—eau is pronounced 'oh')

p   pea

q   queue/cue

r   hour (timer)

s   ass

t   tea

u   U-boat (German submarine)

v   feet

w   bubble

x   eggs

y   wine

z   zebra.

Just read the list aloud a couple of times and picture each letter reminder briefly and you will have it memorised.

Example: Using the alphabet reminders

Let's use the reminders to remember correct spelling of words that may trouble us—remember to concentrate and fix the image of the object or what's happening in your memory.

- *Absence* is spelt with an E and a C. All of the *eels* are *absent* from the *sea*. Or, someone has stolen the money from the charity tin—all of the p*ence* are missing (absent). Either picture will remind you of the correct spelling of absence.

- *Professor*—does it have one or two Fs? There is only one *ref* in a boxing ring and he is a professor. Or, I picture con*fess*ing to my pro*fess*or. You have a choice of methods or, better still, use both to reinforce the spelling in your mind.

- *Lose* and *loose*—how would you remember the spelling for these two? Here are some suggestions if you get stuck, but try it for yourself first. The word 'lose' has obviously *lost* an O and the h*oo*d is l*oo*se and keeps falling off your head. You could picture a n*oo*se not doing its job because it is l*oo*se or the w*oo*den handle of an axe is loose and the head keeps flying off.

Key points

- To remember the spelling of a new word, join or link the word you are learning to an easy word you already know how to spell.

- If you don't know the rule, you'll need a reminder.

- Use the alphabet reminders to help with remembering the spelling of tricky words.

- Learning some simple spelling rules can help you with the spelling of many words.

 More activities to try

- What words do you get wrong or misspell? Even the word 'misspell' can be tricky. It has a double S. You can remember it if you think that Miss Pell can't spell.

- Make your own spelling list either in the back of one of your exercise books or in a notebook that you keep in your schoolbag. When you get a word wrong, write it in your notebook with a way to remember the spelling for next time. Remember: use a word you know to help you spell words you don't know.

Chapter 6
How to solve problems like a genius

Have you ever had a really difficult problem and, because you had no idea what to do, you went to a friend or an adult you trusted and asked for their advice? Did you discover that, when you finished explaining the problem, you didn't need to ask for an answer because you already knew what you should do? Explaining the problem to someone else was enough to tell you what you should do.

The power of visualising

Seeing your problem in your mind and seeing the outcome you want will often give you the clue you need to get the outcome you want. If somebody gives me a task and I am not sure how to do it, I will 'see' myself doing it, and that will often tell me what I need to do the job. Athletes are taught to visualise themselves winning before they actually perform. See yourself kicking the goal before you kick the ball.

Seeing yourself sitting an exam could tell you that you need pencils, a sharpener, a calculator and backups in case something goes wrong.

The ability to visualise is not only useful for study and for learning information. The ability can help in other areas of your life. It is a very useful skill to develop. You can use it to achieve what you want in life. Seeing yourself getting what you want will often give you the clue that you need for understanding how to achieve the things you want to do.

Visualising can allow you to solve logic puzzles. Let's look at some examples.

Example: A tall man and a short man

Who can reach higher, a short man standing on the shoulders of a tall man or a tall man standing on the shoulders of a short man?

See the two pictures in your mind and you will easily see the answer.

Which man has longer arms to reach higher?

As we have already discovered, your imagination is a powerful tool.

I will put the answer at the end of the chapter so you can check your answer. If you actually *see* the men you will have the answer.

Example: Rafael in Nicaragua

Here is a puzzle that illustrates how effective visualisation can be in solving problems and puzzles.

Rafael is in jail in Nicaragua. He is going to be executed in the morning. He looks around the cell for some way to escape before the sentence is carried out. The only piece of furniture is a bed attached to the wall. It can't be moved. The cell has a dirt floor, but the walls go several feet below ground level. They go down too far for Rafael to tunnel under.

He looks at the barred skylight in the middle of the ceiling. It has a strong lock on it but Rafael knows that if he can reach it he can unlock it. There is no furniture to drag under it and it is too high to reach. He can't reach the skylight by jumping, although he tries but fails. His only tool is a metal cup he uses for drinking.

He digs a hole in the floor using his cup and climbs out through the skylight. How does he do it?

If you can't solve it, pretend you are Rafael and stuck in the cell. *See* yourself, actually *see yourself* in your mind, digging the hole and climbing through the skylight. How did you do it?

Many people who attend my learning programs know the answer to this problem immediately, but others don't. When I ask them to pretend they are Rafael and *see* themselves digging the hole and climbing out through the skylight, their faces light up as the answer dawns: they dig a hole and make a mound from the pile of dirt dug out. They stand on the mound and reach the skylight. Visualisation can be a powerful tool for solving problems.

Some people visualise as a matter of course, but many never do. With practice, you can develop the ability to visualise and you can develop the habit. And using the reminders can be very helpful here.

Using reminders develops creative thinking skills

Each time you use the methods taught in this book, you develop your thinking skills in three ways:

1 You have to determine the picture connection you will make between the reminder and the information you are learning. Because we have a rule that the connection should be ridiculous, you are learning to think creatively and outside the box. You are developing lateral thinking skills.

2 Seeing the picture of the object, or what is happening, develops your ability to visualise. You need to *see* the picture in as much detail as you can to improve your memory of it.

3 Making the pictures develops your concentration, because you can't do the first two steps without a high level of concentration.

I have taught people who have suffered brain damage in traffic accidents and were told by their doctors they would never again be able to concentrate in the way they could before the accident. As they used these methods, their concentration improved until they were accomplishing more than they ever did before their accidents. They quickly improved the level and the length of concentration they could achieve and were able to learn at a level they would never have dreamed possible before.

Courses on creative thinking and concentration

I have read books about creative thinking and attended workshops that teach you to visualise and think outside the square. We were given a lot of drills and exercises to practise at home after the program to develop our skills. I haven't found anyone who actually did the exercises. It seemed too much like hard work.

If you are asked to perform exercises to improve your ability to think creatively, you will probably give up after a while. Performing exercises requires willpower and a high level of commitment.

When you use the reminder method you aren't performing exercises to improve your mind—you are using the reminders to remember what you have to pick up from the supermarket, to remember an argument you need to present, to study for an exam or to perform better in school. You are using the reminders to make your life easier. It isn't a system of performing boring exercises.

And each time you make a connection you are developing your creative thinking skills because we are making strange, ridiculous connections between unrelated objects. By definition, you are thinking outside the square. This is an important exercise to develop creative or lateral thinking skills. But without the motivation for learning, making the ridiculous connections just to develop your skills seems too much like hard work to most people, so they give up.

I have found that students who are studying for exams will use my methods and apply them to what they are studying. My methods don't add to their workload—on the contrary, they lighten the workload. Students find that the methods work so they keep using them. So, I believe these study methods give better results than the high-priced creative thinking programs.

Key points

- Lateral thinking exercises can be boring. Using your imagination to remember what you need will get better results.

- You can apply this book's visualisation and reminder methods to your personal problems and puzzles, not just your schoolwork.

- Use the visualisation and reminder methods to achieve your own goals and personal success.

- Truly *seeing* the problem is the first step to solving the problem or learning the new information.

- Talking the problem through is often enough to help you solve the problem because describing the problem makes you concentrate on really *seeing* it.

More activities to try

Here are some more puzzles for you to try. The ability to make good pictures in your mind will help you solve them. See how you go. Don't be too quick to give up.

⟳ Two traffic police are waiting for speeding motorists. One cop is looking up the highway, the other is looking down it so they cover all of the lanes. One says to the other, 'Mike, what are you smiling about?' How could he tell that Mike was smiling?

⟳ A woman gave a beggar 50 cents. She is the beggar's sister but the beggar is not the woman's brother. How are they related?

⟳ How can you throw a ball as hard as you can and have it stop and come back to you without the ball hitting anything?

⟳ Five criminals rode 50 km to their hideout. Nobody noticed they drove the whole way with a flat tyre. How come?

The answers are overleaf.

Answers

The tall man/short man problem

If a tall man stands on the shoulders of a short man, his head will be at the same height as a small man standing on the shoulders of a tall man. So, the difference lies in the reach of the man on top. The tall man will have longer arms than the short man, so if he is standing on top of the short man he will be able to reach higher than the short man could.

Extra activities

- The police officers were facing each other.
- The beggar is the woman's sister.
- Throw the ball straight up in the air.
- The flat tyre was the spare.

Chapter 7
How to write like a genius

A student came to me in tears for his after-school lesson. He was clearly very upset and it took a while for him to actually say what the problem was.

A week before, he had asked me for help in writing essays. He told me that he simply couldn't express himself and his teacher ridiculed his essays. 'They are just no good', he said. Could I help?

I gave him the advice I give you in this chapter. He followed the advice when he wrote his next essay. When the teacher handed the essays back with the grades, he saw his teacher had written on it in red, 'Write the essay again, and this time write it yourself!'

He was devastated, but I assured him this was the highest compliment he could have been paid. His teacher had seen such an improvement in his work that he couldn't believe the boy had written it himself.

Many people panic when they are asked to write an essay or a report. Here are some simple rules to follow that will greatly improve your essays and written assignments. First we'll talk about how to write an essay where you must persuade the reader or present an argument, then look at the kind of essay that needs storytelling.

How to write to present an argument or persuasive essay

Examples of a persuasive essay are subjects like 'Why I think school should begin an hour later in the morning' or 'Why I like reading books' or 'Why we should or shouldn't learn a foreign language in school'.

Here are the seven steps:

1 Plan what you want to say and how you will say it.

2 Begin with an attention-getter.

3 State what you want to accomplish, or what you want to convince the reader of or what you want the reader to do or change.

4 Set out your arguments clearly, and deal with them one at a time.

5 Give illustrations and examples.

6 Summarise what you have written.

7 Finish with what you want the reader to do or believe.

1 Plan what you want to say and how you will say it

Let's assume you have been given a subject to write about or you have decided on one yourself. If you are choosing your own topic, what do you feel strongly about? Or what would you like to see changed? Or what are the things you really enjoy?

Now you have decided on your subject, think about what you already know about it. Write that down. What more can you find out about it? Try a Google search and look up the topic on Wikipedia. Get as much background information as you can.

What do you think about the question? Why? Write down your reasons for your beliefs about the subject as a list. Can you think of any stories or examples to illustrate your points?

Write down all the points you can think of that show why you think you are right. At this stage write an outline of the essay. Write the main points and maybe a couple of notes under each heading to remind you to include thoughts as they occur to you.

2 Begin with an attention-getter

Here are some attention-getters that would make good opening sentences for this kind of essay. One of the reasons they work is that you can tell from the first sentence exactly what the essay is going to be about.

'Did you know that one in three people over the age of 10 can't read?'

'The countries went to war because an interpreter made a simple mistake in his translation.'

'Our school is in danger of closing if we can't get government funding.'

'What do you call a person who speaks three languages? Trilingual.

'What do you call a person who speaks two languages? Bilingual.

'What do you call a person who speaks one language? An Australian.'

If readers aren't persuaded to keep reading by the first sentence of your essay, they probably won't. You need to say something or ask a question that will force the reader to look for more. Achieve this in an exam and you are well on your way to a pass.

Try saying something controversial, outrageous or that contradicts what everyone is saying or believing.

Or tell an interesting story that will get the reader's attention. A story is often the most effective way to get the reader's full attention—we all love a story. Tell a story that highlights the arguments you are going to make.

'I was standing at a bus stop in Germany and a man was standing on the road talking to his friends with his back to the traffic. He didn't see the bus coming behind him and the driver didn't appear to see him. I wanted to warn him so I tried to think of the German for "Look out" and, while I was trying to remember, the bus hit him. It only grazed his shoulder but it could have been much worse.'

That is actually a true story and it gets people's full attention.

3 State what you want to accomplish

What are you trying to accomplish? What do you want the reader to do? What do you want your readers to believe? Do you want to convince them of something, or persuade them to take action or change? Tell them what you want. Tell them why they should do it.

'Everyone should be able to read at a basic level.'

'Everyone should learn at least one foreign language.'

'There is the story of the German sitting in an English restaurant calling to the waiter, "When do I become a sausage?" The word *bekommen* in German means to receive. This is a humorous mistake but not understanding foreign languages can lead to some serious misunderstandings.'

'A Frenchman once said that he demanded his soldiers be able to control the border. The word *demander* in French means to ask and *controller* means to watch closely and observe change. The English soldiers didn't like his "demand".'

4 Set out your arguments clearly, and deal with them one at a time

In your planning notes, number the arguments and points you want to make. Then, write each argument, one at a time. Are the arguments valid? Would you be convinced if you read them? Do you believe your own arguments? If an argument is weak, leave it out. Just write why you believe what you do.

Don't overwhelm the reader with too many arguments. Just give a few of what you think are your strongest arguments.

Tip

Keep your points simple and give only the strongest reasons. Don't give too many or you might confuse the reader.

5 Give illustrations and examples

Illustrate your points with examples. People forget dry arguments, but they do remember stories. And people like to read stories. A story gets the reader's attention. A good story can turn the result in your favour. A story will also be more persuasive if you are trying to change someone's mind.

'The government tried to close our school in the 1980s, but the students and parents staged protests and ran barbecues in the main street and saved the school from closing. They wrote to the newspapers and got onto talkback radio. The government backed down.'

'When we were in Bali we didn't understand the sign warning us of danger.'

'When we were in China we couldn't tell which was the boys' or girls' toilet because we couldn't read the signs on the doors.'

'Accidents happen when parents drop off their children at school in the morning because they have to compete on the roads with people driving to work.'

6 Summarise what you have written

When you finish, summarise your main points in one or two sentences. Remind the readers of what they have just read and why they should agree with you.

'School needs to start an hour later so kids can get more sleep and perform better in class. It is also safer for kids because there is less traffic on the roads.'

7 Finish with what you want your reader to do or believe

Remember, you are trying to argue a point and persuade the reader to agree with your point of view. Tell the reader what you want him or her to do. Don't lose sight of that. You might finish with:

'Let's talk to the school administration and picket the mayor's office.'

'Let's talk to the school administration about a later start.'

'Let's all learn another language, even if it is not part of the school program.'

'Let's have special programs for problem readers.'

'Let's find out why the current methods aren't working.'

Using the reminders to generate ideas

You can also use the reminder system we have already talked about to generate ideas for your essay. I see it as using the reminders in reverse. What arguments do the reminders bring to mind?

Your teacher has given you an assignment to write an essay on why you love your parents. You might be saying to yourself, 'What is there to write about? Of course I love my parents. You have to love your parents—that's how the system works. I have no idea what to write. I don't know where to start.'

Let's see how you can use your reminders to generate ideas.

1 We begin with one, run. Picture yourself running with your parents. You say to yourself, 'We are playing a game.' Okay, that is your first point: your parents play with you.

2 How about the next reminder, two, shoe? That one is easy. You see your parents buying you shoes. They buy your clothes.

So, number one, run, they play with you; and two, shoe, they clothe you.

3 Three, tree. You see your family swinging from branch to branch like monkeys on the tree in your yard. That doesn't help much. You can't say you love your parents because they act like monkeys, can you? Well, why not? Then you think about the tree in your yard and how you have stood beneath the branches when it has rained to try to keep dry.

Your parents have given you shelter. You live in a cosy house and have a roof over your head. That is number three.

4 Four, door. You see the door to your room in your imagination, then you see the front door of your house. Your door protects you from the people outside. You see yourself running from bullies who want to hurt you and you slam the door in their faces so they can't get you. Four, door, reminds you that your parents protect you.

5 Five is hive. You picture a beehive with bees buzzing around. The bees sting you. I love my parents because they sting me? That won't work. As you look at the hive in your imagination you see the hive producing honey. My parents feed me.

6 Six is sticks, and you see your parents punishing you when you need it. Your parents teach you right and wrong. My parents give me standards. They encourage me to have high standards and to always do what is right.

7 Seven, heaven is easy. My parents teach me values. They give me beliefs or religious instruction and a foundation for my life. Again, they teach me right and wrong, but they also teach me to aim for the highest with my life.

8 Eight, gate doesn't inspire any ideas, but I feel I already have plenty to write about. Nine and ten give me no new ideas either, because I already have the points that my parents feed me, which seem the obvious ideas from dine and hen.

Now you can not only write your essay, but you could also give a talk on the subject to your class without using any notes. You have memorised the points.

You would certainly have memorised the points if you used this method to write your essay, but you have probably memorised the points by simply reading them.

Call back the points of why you love your parents, from one to seven.

I have used this method to generate ideas for talks. I have my listeners memorise the talk as I give it and then call it back from memory afterwards.

The reminders gave me an easy way to generate the ideas I needed for my talk, and meant that everyone was concentrating during the talk as I had them make the mental pictures.

How to write a story essay

Writing a story essay, such as 'My Birthday Party' or 'My Holiday in Queensland', has its own rules. They are:

1 Begin with an attention-getter.

2 Explain the events that led up to the opening paragraph.

3 Use plenty of dialogue.

4 Use adjectives (adjectives describe the nouns).

5 Use adverbs to describe the action (adverbs add more information to the adjectives and verbs).

6 Finish quickly and neatly.

1 Begin with an attention-getter

The story doesn't have to begin at the beginning. Start the story with the most exciting event in your story to grab the reader's attention and then describe the events that led up to it. Here are some attention-getting sentences that might work in a story essay:

'My sister was sick across the table.'

'The undertow swept me off my feet and took me out to sea.'

'The undertow swept me off my feet and I was certain I was going to drown.'

2 Explain the events that led up to the opening paragraph

Your next sentence, to explain what you said in your first sentence, might be:

'This was the first time my mother had let me invite my friends to my birthday party.'

'We were on holidays on the Gold Coast and I wanted to swim at a surf beach.'

3 Use plenty of dialogue

Explain some action and feelings of participants through dialogue. That is much more compelling than just describing what happened without any speech. People find dialogue more interesting and easier to read. Dialogue also fires the imagination. You might say:

'Let me see those.'

'You don't have to snatch them from me! I want you to see them.'

4 Use adjectives

Use adjectives (words that describe nouns or other adjectives) to bring your story to life and enable the reader to experience and see what you are writing. Use words like slow, quick, awkward, gaudy, sluggish, rough, smooth, shiny, slippery or furry to conjure a picture in the reader's mind. For example: an old unpainted house.

Adjectives encourage and enable the reader to make a vivid mental picture of the events, and, as we know, strong visuals help us understand and remember what is happening.

5 Use adverbs to describe the action

Adverbs describe the verbs and adjectives. They tell how something was done. Some examples are stealthily, silently, deftly, noisily, awkwardly, happily, hungrily, angrily. This adds to the reader's mental picture of what you have written.

6 Finish quickly and neatly

'Next time I'll know not to invite my sister—or at least put the cream cakes at the other end of the table.'

'My father said, "No more swimming for you except between the flags. And only when one of us is with you."

'I agreed.'

Practise writing essays on your own to try out these methods. Try writing both kinds of essays just for your own enjoyment. You will find you get better with practice.

The rules for writing good essays are simple. Follow them and you will improve your results.

Good grammar

Here are some basics in English grammar that will help with many tricky problems you might come across when you are writing essays. You will find whole books written about English grammar but this should help you with some of the most common mistakes people make.

Apostrophes

Apostrophes have two main uses:

- to indicate missing letters
- to show possession

Missing letters

We often write 'I'm' instead of 'I am' and 'can't' instead of 'cannot'. The apostrophe tells us we have left out some letters.

Sometimes there are words that sound alike but must be spelled differently because they mean different things: 'you're' and 'your' are two examples.

'You're' is short for 'you are' (it's called a contraction). We would say, 'You're going tonight', which means 'you are going tonight'. It is not, 'Your going tonight.' 'Your' means 'belongs to you'. For instance, 'this is your hat'.

But we don't need an apostrophe in most singular verbs that say he, she or it did something. Some examples are 'he wants', 'she sees' or 'it runs'.

Sometimes you will see words like 'he want's', 'she see's' or 'it run's on signs or in writing. But they are wrong. (Look out and see how many wrong ones you can find.)

Its and it's — a tricky one

'It's' is short for 'It is', showing that something has been left out. You could say, 'It's coloured red', meaning 'it is coloured red'.

'Its', with no apostrophe, shows possession or ownership. For instance, 'red is its colour'.

You could say, 'It's coloured red—red is its colour'. Written in full would be, 'It is coloured red—red is its colour'.

Possession

People often get confused using an apostrophe to show ownership or possession. This is Jim's hat. This is Jane's scarf. This is the dog's kennel. In each case, the person or thing (Jim, Jane, the dog) owned the object, and we show that with the apostrophe and the 's'.

When the object or objects belong to more than one person or thing, the apostrophe goes *after* the 's'. Here are some examples.

'The boy's clothes' means one boy's clothes. (The clothes of one boy, so the apostrophe goes before the 's'.)

'The boys' clothes' means several boys' clothes. (The clothes of *more than* one boy, so the apostrophe goes *after* the 's'.)

'The girl's ribbons' means one girl's ribbons.

'The girls' ribbons' means several girls' ribbons

'The bank's customers' means one bank's customers.

'The banks' customers' means several banks' customers.

If the plural ends in an 's', you place the apostrophe after it. If it doesn't end in an 's', like men, women and children, you place the apostrophe before the 's'. Here are some examples: men's clothing, women's shoes, children's toys.

No apostrophe in plurals

When we add an 's' to make something plural (show there is more than one of the item), we don't need an apostrophe. When you see words like 'red apple's' or 'exercise book's', or 'the pen's', the writer got it wrong—there's no possession or missing letters to show. Again, if you look out you will find plenty of examples of these errors, especially on signs.

Affect or effect

'Affect' is a *verb* which means it does something: for example, 'the books you read will affect the way you think'.

'Effect' is a *noun*. You can talk about *the* effect or *an* effect. For instance, 'The crowd's booing had an *effect* on the way she played'. Or, you could say, 'the booing *affected* the way she played'.

Less or fewer

'Less' refers to *quantity*: 'there is *less water* in the dams this year'.

'Fewer' refers to *numbers*: 'there were *fewer injuries* after we watered the playing area'.

Here are two more examples: 'people drink *less milk* than they did 10 years ago', and '*fewer people* suffer from the plague now, and they spend *less time* in hospital'.

Fewer means not as many (it goes with a plural noun, such as 'injuries') and less means not as much (it goes with a singular noun, like 'water').

You and I, or you and me

Is it 'Jim and me went to the beach', or 'Jim and I went to the beach'?

Is it, 'You and I can do it' or 'You and me can do it'?

Is it 'It is the same for you and I' or 'It is the same for you and me?'

Is there an easy way to know? Yes. If you drop the 'Jim and', the 'you and' and the 'you and' from each of the sentences above, you can tell whether you should say 'me' or 'I' in the sentence.

Let's look at the example of 'It is the same for you and I'.

If we drop the 'you and' and leave the 'I', we get:

'It is the same for me.'

'It is the same for I.'

'It is the same for me' sounds correct, but 'It is the same for I' does not sound right.

Now let's look at 'Jim and me went home'. We drop the 'Jim and' to leave 'me went home'. This is obviously wrong, so the sentence should be 'Jim and I went home'.

Another rule to help you remember is that 'you and me' always follows a preposition. It is always 'for you and me', 'to you and me' 'between you and me' and 'before you and me' and 'after you and me'.

Key points

- Open your essay with a startling statement or a story to grab the reader's attention.

- Your story-telling doesn't have to start at the beginning.

- Use the number reminder system to help you develop ideas for your essay.

- Remember the seven steps for writing the two kinds of essay.

- Use direct speech in a story-telling essay to make the action more engaging.

More activities to try

- ✍ Use these suggestions next time you have to write an essay for school.

- ✍ Write an essay on the most exciting event in your life.

- ✍ Write an essay to persuade your classmates to pool their money to buy you the birthday present you want.

Chapter 8
How to summarise information like a genius

One of my daughters came home from school very upset.

'Please write a note for me,' she cried. 'Please tell my English teacher I can't write précis.'

Précis writing is something like what Reader's Digest does to books, only more so. Reader's Digest reduces books to maybe half or two-thirds their size; a précis of the book will reduce the story to only a few pages.

If you write a précis of a magazine article you are writing a summary, outlining what the article is saying. If the article presents an argument, a précis will give a summary of the arguments but will include them all. A précis of a story will give the outline of the story but leave out most of the detail.

I asked my daughter what the assignment was. She said she had to write a précis or summary of the Henry Lawson story 'The Loaded Dog'. I knew we had the story on the bookshelf, so I asked her to get it.

She said, 'Yes, but I still can't write précis.'

'That's okay. Just get the book.'

She got the book and opened to the story. I said, 'Read the first paragraph.'

'All right, but I still can't write précis.'

She read the first paragraph.

Then I said to her, 'Use the reminder system to memorise it.' My daughter knew I was asking her to memorise what the paragraph was saying—not to memorise it word for word. She had to analyse what the paragraph said and then memorise her summary. Maybe the paragraph could be summed up in two or three words.

'I've done it.'

'Now read the second paragraph and memorise it.'

Then she read the third and the fourth paragraph and memorised them, and so on until we got to the end of the story.

'Now, tell me what was the first paragraph about.'

She told me in one sentence.

'Good, write it down. What was the second paragraph about?'

She told me again—this time in two sentences. She wrote it down.

'What was the third paragraph?'

She told me in one sentence.

I said, 'Write it down.'

'I am writing a précis, aren't I?'

'Exactly.'

No one had ever told her *how* to write a précis. She was capable of writing a summary—she just needed guidance to show her how to do it. Anything seems hard to us if we don't know how to go about it or where to start. This was a method that my daughter could easily understand. I have taught this method around the world and many students have told me it has made it easy for them.

Using the reminders to write a summary

Using the reminder system to learn actually helps you also develop the skills you need to write a précis or summary. It teaches you to analyse what you are reading: what is the article or story actually telling me? What is it saying? When you have to write a précis, you are reading to get the meaning. You are reading for a deeper understanding than when you just read a novel for fun.

The reminder system helps you to summarise what you have read by joining the new information (the story) to the information you already know (the reminder system). You join the summary to the reminder and, if you have understood the passage, you can call back a summary of what it is saying. Concentrating on associating the story with the reminders helps you understand it. Putting the passage into your own words is really summarising what you have read.

It can be fun to read a magazine article and memorise the article as you read. You only memorise an outline: you don't memorise it word for word. Then call back the points you have memorised. This forces you to analyse what you are reading. You can't memorise a point if you don't understand it. This is active learning as opposed to passive learning. It is also active reading as opposed to passive reading. You are doing more than just seeing the words on the page. Try it with a magazine or newspaper article now.

Now write down your summary, and you have written a précis of the article.

Key points

- A précis summarises the key points of a story or article.

- Use the reminders to analyse, summarise and memorise what you read.

- Replace each paragraph in the story or article with one or two sentences for the précis.

- Writing a summary is just another way of writing notes.

More activities to try

- The next time you read a magazine article or a chapter in a book that you like, memorise it using the reminders. If you found it really helpful, put it all in your permanent memory. That way, you can bring back the information any time you like.

- Write a summary of what your teacher says in one of your classes.

- Find a copy of Henry Lawson's story 'The Loaded Dog'. Write your own summary of it.

- Write a summary of this chapter.

Chapter 9
How to speak like a genius

When I was a student in teachers college we had to give an oral presentation to our class. We were allowed to choose our own subject. We were allowed to use notes for an outline, but we weren't allowed to read our presentation. I was surprised how nervous some students became—we were speaking to our friends. The students were adults, but they were more than nervous—they were terrified.

I remember one student in particular. Some weeks before another student had asked him between classes whether butter or margarine was better, and he told the whole class what he thought. He was very forceful and I still remember some of the points he made. But when he had to give a formal presentation his voice took on a nervous quality and he was shaking with fear—even though he was speaking to the same people.

It has been said that the fear of public speaking is one of the greatest fears known to humans—especially among adults. It is also one of the most useful skills you can have in life.

When we came to give our presentations, the students who did best spoke on issues they felt strongly about. The enthusiasm of the speaker was catching and we were soon involved in what the speaker had to say. The lesson is to speak from the heart and people will listen.

Don't read your speech. Nothing turns people off more quickly than to listen to someone reading from a piece of paper. Using the reminders can enable you to speak without notes. Here are my tips for giving a good talk.

Some rules for giving a good talk

There are six simple rules you can follow when you are preparing and giving a talk, whatever the subject is. Here they are:

1 Open with an attention-getter—just like the attention-getters we talked about in chapter 7. Tell a story that introduces your subject or give some surprising fact to spark your listeners' interest.

2 Plan your talk. Decide beforehand what points you want to make. Are you trying to get your audience to believe something or take some action? Are you trying to educate your audience on how they can achieve some goal? Decide what your aim is and then make sure your talk achieves what you want.

3 Use the reminders to memorise the main points of your talk. Point one (run) is your opening story or surprising fact. Point two (shoe) might outline what you want to achieve. Points three, four and five might be your instructions or arguments, point six your summary and point seven your conclusion.

4 Your conclusion, or close, should be some kind of call to action or a challenge, to get your audience to do something to make a change. If your talk was purely to inform or entertain, then simply summarise what you have said.

5 You only need to memorise the main points—not your whole talk. If you know your stuff you will easily fill in details.

6 Include examples and stories to illustrate. People forget facts and arguments but they will remember your stories. If someone's attention is beginning to wander, a story will quickly bring them back.

American author Mark Twain was a gifted speaker as well as a great writer, and he decided early on to speak without notes. He tells how he used rhyming word reminders to be able to speak while he moved around the podium and looked directly at his listeners, not at his notes. Your audience will see you as a more forceful speaker and as more authoritative—someone who really knows their stuff—if you speak without notes.

I had to give an after-dinner talk and I wasn't happy with the talk I had prepared. I changed my subject to one I thought would be more interesting for my audience, and then I used my reminders to come up with ideas for my points. I spoke about the 10 secrets of success and used the rhyming reminders. When I gave the talk I had the audience memorise each point as I gave it using the same reminders and pictures I had used. The audience loved it. One, run, reminded them to set goals. You won't achieve anything if you don't know what you want. I told them to picture they were running into an open goal and kicked the winning goal for their team. They were able to repeat my talk months later. So, in this case the reminders not only helped me plan the talk, they enabled me to speak without notes and then the audience was able to remember the talk months later.

We can use the reminders to create ideas as well as memorise them. We used the same idea in chapter 7 to create ideas for our essay.

Speaker's nerves

The reminder system can also help if you suffer a bout of speaker's nerves. You suddenly panic in the middle of your presentation. You realise you have lost track of what you are saying and your mind isn't working. You are embarrassed and just want to disappear through the floor. When this happens, just take a slow drink of water. This accounts for the fact you have stopped speaking. No one expects you to keep talking while you are drinking. (If there is no water on the podium, simply ask someone to get you a glass: 'Can somebody get me a drink of water please?')

While you are waiting or drinking, go through your reminders:

- One, run—we covered that.

- Two, shoe—I have spoken about that.

- Three, tree—Yes, I was speaking on that.

- Four, door—I haven't begun on point four so I will do that now.

Remember, making the pictures in your mind forces high concentration. You can't concentrate on your mental pictures and your fear at the same time. Using the reminders puts you in control of your emotions.

So you continue with point four. Don't worry if you haven't finished point three. No one will know anyway.

Speaking without notes and making an orderly presentation, point by point, will make you stand out as someone way above the rest of the class.

Key points

- Use the reminders to overcome speaker's nerves.

- Speak without notes — people will be impressed.

- Start with an attention-getter.

- Use stories and examples to illustrate your points.

- Conclude with a call to action or a summary of your talk.

More activities to try

- ☝ Use these suggestions the next time you give a class presentation.

- ☝ Plan a talk on your favourite subject just in case you are called to speak without warning.

- ☝ Use the reminder system to plan a talk on why you enjoy your hobby.

- ☝ Plan a talk about your pet if you have one. Use the reminders to plan, and then to give your talk, without notes.

Chapter 10
How to learn a language like a genius

I have always been intrigued by the idea of learning another language. Long before I ever went to school, I wanted to be able to speak in a language that none of my friends or family could understand. I saw it as a means of secret communication.

When I discovered that the girls who lived next door learned French at school I begged them to teach me French. They were only too happy to play school in the backyard and give me lessons. They wrote the lessons on a blackboard and gave me written notes, although I was too young to read. I retained what they had taught me up until the time I started high school and took my own French classes.

Since I left school I have learned more at night classes and with home study courses than I ever did at school. I have come to the conclusion that I could have learnt the equivalent of six years' school French in just six months by myself — and I became a language addict.

I have written about learning languages in more detail in my book, *Fast, Easy Way to Learn a Language* (published by John Wiley & Sons Australia, 2005; you can get a copy from me at www.speedmathematics.com), but I will outline my basic method here.

Fast, easy way to learn a language

First, buy a kids' learning program to use at home for the language you want to learn. There are some excellent programs that include books and recordings to use at home, and some excellent computer programs that allow you to play with the language. Kidspeak is a great children's program for home study. It is a computer program with games and activities to teach the basics of the language. Kids find it fun. It is produced by Transparent Language and available from their website, www.transparent.com.

I highly recommend the Assimil Language Courses®. Assimil® courses will take you to a high level of fluency, and they are suitable for both younger and older students. They follow a two-stage approach to learning languages and the lessons are broken up so that each one represents an easy amount to learn in one day. Each lesson has a humorous cartoon to illustrate what you have learned and the lessons are written in ordinary spoken language with humour to make learning pleasant. They recommend you read and listen to each lesson until you simply understand it. You don't have to worry about committing anything to memory or about learning conjugations or grammar. The second stage is an active phase, where you go back 50 lessons (equal to 50 days) and translate from your own language to the new language and you do some exercises. By this time you find the whole process to be simple. I have bought Assimil® courses for more than a dozen languages. I love them.

I also recommend the two-wave approach to learning languages taught by Assimil® in my book. Move ahead as fast as you can through your school textbook and then, when you have reached chapter 5 or 6, go back to the first chapter and work through the exercises. You will find it easy because you have become familiar with the words and the grammar. Don't memorise the grammar—try to learn it simply by using it. That's the way you learned the grammar for your own language.

Play with the language

Here are some ways you can practise your new language by playing with it:

- Talk to yourself in the language.

- Read comics or joke books in your new language.

- Read magazines in your new language on topics that interest you.

- Listen to music sung in in your new language. Try to find the words to the songs on the internet.

- Watch movies in the language you are learning. With DVDs you can watch the movie in your own language with foreign subtitles or watch it in a foreign language with subtitles in your own language. When you are familiar with the language you can watch the DVD with both sound and subtitles in the target language so you can both hear and read the language you are learning. Next time you buy a DVD, check the language options on the back.

When I am learning a new language, I also plan for immersion days or half-days when I can immerse myself in the language. I plan to follow some language lessons, do some reading, watch a movie and listen to music, and also eat food from a country where they speak the language. I might also visit a club or organisation where everyone speaks the language I am learning.

Using the link system to learn vocabulary

There is a saying in Europe that you have to learn a word and forget it seven times before you have learned it properly. We can eliminate most of the effort and frustration of learning a foreign vocabulary by using our linking method to learn a useful vocabulary in record time.

When I say to make a mental picture, remember to concentrate and actually do it. Don't just agree with the picture—see it in your mind. This forces a high degree of concentration. This forces active learning instead of passive learning, which we talked about in chapter 1.

Here are some examples of using linking to learn vocabulary in three different languages.

Learn some French vocab

Cochon means pig. How do we remember that? *Cochon* sounds like cushion. We join the sound-alike, cushion, to the meaning, pig. I picture having small pigs on my lounge instead of cushions and I tell my visitors, pull up a pig and take a seat. That reminds me of the meaning of *cochon*. It tells me that *cochon* is French for pig.

Livre is French for book. I picture that I always *leave* my book behind when I go to school. I always forget to take it with me. I join *livre* with *leave*. Make a mental picture of leaving your book behind and someone running after you to give it to you, and you have it memorised.

Voudrais is an important word to learn. *Je voudrais* means 'I would like'. *Voudrais* sounds like *food tray*. If you are hungry you can picture yourself saying, 'I would like a food tray'. And it is a phrase you would use often so it will quickly go into your permanent memory.

Lait (pronounced lay) is French for milk. I picture cows laying cartons of milk in the same way that hens lay eggs. *See it* and you will remember the French word for milk.

There are a lot of words that are similar in French and English so you will find many words are close enough to remind you of the meanings, like *la table* (the table), *la cassette* (the cassette), *le disc* (the disc) or *la lampe* (the lamp). Be careful, not every word in French means the same in English. For instance, *demander* doesn't mean to demand but to ask.

Learn some German essentials

English is a Germanic language so German is not too difficult for English speakers. Many words sound the same or similar, like Hand (hand), Fuss (foot), Haus (house), and even Strasse for street is not far removed. Verbs like gehen (go), kommen (come) and sagen (say) are also easy to remember because they sound alike in both languages.

Komm her means come here. We have a head start, but we still have a large vocabulary to learn.

Hemd is German for shirt. The *hems* on all of my *shirts* are frayed. Picture your shirts with frayed hems and you have it.

Tisch means table. *Tisch* sounds like *dish*. Imagine a huge dish with legs and you use it as your kitchen table. Picture it.

Kissen means pillow. Picture *kissing* your *pillow*. (*Küssen* means to kiss—close enough that you don't need a reminder. Just don't mix it up with *Kissen*.)

Teller means plate. Your bank *teller* always hands you your money on a *plate*. See yourself at the bank and the teller is handing you your money on a plate.

Tip

Revise your memorised list within five minutes of committing it to memory.

Now try learning some Indonesian words

Here are some Indonesian words to show the method doesn't only work for European languages.

Sudah means already. *Sudah* sounds like Sue ta or Sudan. Your mother says, 'Say ta (thank you) to Sue' (Sue ta) and you reply, 'I already said it'.

Makan means to eat. I am hungry so I will make an omelette. *Make an* sounds like *makan*. It is a bit weak, but we will only need to remember this for a couple of minutes until we revise it.

Boleh means to be able. I am *able* to dance *ballet*. See yourself dancing ballet and saying to someone you *are able to* dance ballet.

Baik (pronounced bike) means good. I simply picture I am a *good bike* rider or I have just received a good bike worth thousands of dollars as a present.

Test yourself

Let's see if this method has worked for you.

- What is French for pig?
- What is French for book?
- What is French for I would like?
- What is French for milk?

- What is German for shirt?

- What is German for table?

- What is German for pillow?

- What is Indonesian for can or to be able?

- What is Indonesian for already?

- What is Indonesian for the verb to eat?

- What is Indonesian for good?

The fact that you could translate from English to the foreign language means the words have passed into your active vocabulary because you associated each one with a mental picture. It is much easier to recognise a foreign word and remember its meaning than it is to call out the foreign word when you are given an English word to translate. You gave the foreign word from the English. That is impressive. It usually takes time for the words to enter your passive vocabulary and then, with use, pass into your active vocabulary, but you have done this very easily here with three different languages.

To put the words into your long-term memory, just keep revising your lists, making the mental pictures as you need them. After a while you won't need the reminders any more.

This is great if you are studying for an exam.

Example: The results for one student

A student asked me to help him learn a basic Japanese vocabulary using this method. He supplied the words from his textbook and we learnt 150 words and their meanings in an hour and a half—a rate of 100 words per hour. That's an excellent return for the time spent.

Play at languages—don't work at them

I don't believe in working at learning languages. I play with languages and make it a form of enjoyment. It might help to pretend you are learning the language to be a spy or an undercover agent. Find what motivates you and do it.

How would you remember these words?

Here are some new words to learn.

- *bistro* is a Russian word meaning 'fast'

- *chitayet* is Russian for 'read'

- *ringo* is Japanese for 'apple'

Can you use the linking method to memorise these words?

Try it for yourself before you read any further.

Now let's see how you might have linked the words to their meaning.

- A *bistro* serves *fast* food and obviously the name comes from the Russian word.

- I picture *reading* a book late at night and it makes me tired and I say, '*Gee*, (I'm) *tired*' (*chitayet*).

- I picture putting tight-fitting *rings* around *apples* while they are still on the tree and the apple grows above and below the ring. The *ring goes* around the apple.

Isn't that more fun than just reading the list of words to learn and hoping they will stay in your mind?

Test yourself

Now, let's see if the new words have gone into your active vocabulary.

What is the Russian word for 'read'?

How do you say 'apple' in Japanese?

How do you say 'fast' in Russian?

That is the fun way to remember words in the language you are learning.

Learning another language should be an adventure and it should be fun.

Key points

- Use sound-alikes to remember vocabulary.

- Play with the language you are learning.

- Read stuff you enjoy in the language you are learning.

- Watch DVDs in the language you are learning.

- Read comics and joke books in the language you are learning.

- Find someone to practise the language with.

 More activities to try

⟳ Which language are you learning in school? Go on the internet and find websites in the language you are learning. There is some fun stuff to play with in most languages.

⟳ The website www.lonweb.org has a lot of resources for many languages, including short stories written in the language side by side with English.

⟳ Make your own links to memorise the new words in the lessons you are currently learning at school. This will make learning fun instead of hard work.

Chapter 11
How to sit tests like a genius

When I was in grades five and six, Friday was test day. We had the equivalent of an end-of-year exam every Friday in every subject. It not only helped us to excel in our final exams but it also got us used to sitting exams. The tests became almost routine—Friday was just another day. I think our teacher did us a huge favour. Ours was the only class in the school that had the Friday tests, and I am very grateful I was in Mr Adamson's class.

Many students have never learned how to sit for examinations, and many schools no longer conduct exams, so the students never learn how to get their best result. These students may leave the exam room wondering why they gave the answers they did, and think of a lot of things they should have written down, if only they had thought of them *during* the exam.

Here are some suggestions for doing your best in an examination.

Before the exam
Being well organised before the exam can make all the difference on exam day.

- Try to have most of your study completed two days before the exam. Spend the day before the exam quietly and revise your notes. Try to avoid panic if you can.

- Have an early night before the examination day. Pack your bag the night before so you are not rushed or panicking in the morning.

- Rise early in the morning and review what you have studied. Make sure you have everything that you will need, and take spare pens, pencils, calculators and anything that could cause problems or a loss of time if they suddenly ran out of ink or stopped functioning.

- Arrive at school in plenty of time—I like to arrive 30 minutes before I have to go into the examination room. Keep conversation with others to a minimum so you aren't distracted, and can prepare your mind and get ready for the exam so you know you are at your mental best.

- While you are waiting to go into the exam room or waiting for the exam to start, you can review your notes one last time using the reminders and seeing the connections, so it is only a matter of minutes between making the links and using them in the exam—they will be fresh in your mind. This will also give you confidence.

 Tip

Use your reminders in the classroom to memorise what you hear as you hear it. Write down your notes for each reminder at the end of the lesson. Use your reminder notes for revision.

Doing the exam

Read the paper through first. Often students are told to do this but they aren't told why. It's a good idea for the following reasons.

- It helps you calm down and puts you in a good frame of mind.

- Often, later questions will suggest answers to earlier questions.

- If you have already read the paper through, while you are answering an early question, the answer to a later question may come to mind. (Make an immediate note for yourself on your paper.)

- Your subconscious mind will often work on the other questions while you are answering another question.

- It also helps you to choose the order you will follow to answer the questions.

- It helps you allocate the time you have to the questions.

Answer the easy questions first. That way you get the marks for what you know early on in the examination. Often, students will work on a difficult question, and spend so much time on the answer that they have no time to answer the easy question that might make the difference between a pass and a fail. Again, the answer to a difficult question can also come to mind while you are answering an easy question, and you are not just sitting there, straining your brain to come up with the answer and losing time.

Make sure you understand the questions. It can be very easy to give an answer you are pleased with that doesn't answer the question you are being asked. If you are in any doubt about what the question means, or what answer the teacher wants because the question seems ambiguous, ask the teacher, if that's possible, or write how you understand the question on the paper. Make a note that if the question has a different meaning, here is your answer in note form.

Leave a question half finished if you get bogged down. Make a note on your test paper of anything you intend to write, and then come back to it later if you have time. If you don't answer the question later, you may still get marks for your outline notes.

Time yourself. Give yourself a certain amount of time for each question or section of the paper. Often, the people who set the paper will have written estimated times for answers on the paper. Work to these estimates as much as possible so you will have as much time as possible for the paper.

Don't waste time padding answers. Teachers usually have strict guidelines for how they allocate marks and they recognise padding when they see it.

If you have time, read the paper through again when you have finished. Make sure you have answered the question, not what you thought the question said, and make sure you have answered all the questions you need to. Try to finish any questions that you didn't finish before.

Examination nerves

Most of us are nervous when we sit an exam. That is good because it makes our mind sharp and alert, and the adrenaline is flowing. But excessive nervousness can prevent us doing our best in an exam. It can get in the way of our thought processes and prevent us answering questions we could easily answer if we were feeling calmer.

Here is where the reminder system of memory can be of immense value. What happens when we find we can't remember an argument or a fact we have learnt? It might be on the tip of our tongue but our nervousness seems to be working against us. What is our usual reaction? We panic: 'I am going to fail.' 'This always happens to me!' 'I knew it would happen.' 'I always get exam nerves.' 'I will have to repeat the year.' Does this sound familiar to you?

This panic doesn't help us recall the information we need: it actually prevents us getting much further. We can't think straight when we panic. But, we have a solution.

What do I need to remember? Argument number three. Tree will remind me of it. I see a tree in my imagination. What is it doing? Where is it? What has happened to it?

While I am making my mental picture, what am I forcing? Total concentration. You can't concentrate on your mental picture and concentrate on your panic at the same time, so using the reminders puts you in control of your emotions and your panic.

Not only are you now in control of your panic but your mental picture has reminded you of the information that was the cause of your panic. It is a double win.

I have talked to many students about this. One student said to the class, 'It is like being in an exam and you can't remember the answer so you turn to your friend and say, "What was number five?" Your friend says, "I can't tell you the answer because that would be cheating, but hive will remind you of the answer."' Everyone in the class said it would be cheating if he did that in the exam, so he said, 'Well, I turn to my *invisible* friend in my mind and he gives me the clue that reminds me of the answer.'

That worried one girl in the class who said, 'Maybe it *is* cheating.' We assured her it isn't cheating, because you come up with the answers yourself.

We can turn sitting exams from a negative to a positive experience. If you know you can't fail, then you don't have the pressure everyone associates with sitting exams.

A student told me that he used the methods in this book to prepare for an exam. He said he felt like laughing out loud as he walked out of the examination room because he said it was so easy. He had never felt that way about an exam before.

Key points

- Revise for exams using the notes you made at the end of a topic.

- Finish revising your work two days before the exam.

- Be organised — pack your bag the night before with everything you need.

- Have spare pens, pencils, rulers, calculators, erasers, and anything else you might need, ready for exam day.

- Get a good night's sleep before an exam and arrive early — don't let yourself be rushed or stressed.

- Using the reminder system is like having a friend in the exam room to prompt you.

Some activities to try

⌂ Make your own exam and then answer your own questions and ask your teacher to mark it. Have your teacher tell you why your answer was either accepted or not accepted. This can give you a better idea of what your teacher wants.

⌂ Use your reminders in the classroom to memorise what you hear as you hear it. Write down your notes for each reminder at the end of the lesson.

⌂ Make a list of things you need to take into an exam.

⌂ If your textbook has questions at the end of each chapter, try answering them and submit your answers to your teacher. This will show you if you understand the subject.

Part III

Some more fun with speed learning

In part III we will look at some fun ways to play with the methods and to show off your skills. They are a good way to practise making mental pictures and developing the creative skills needed to make connections with things that have nothing in common. I have heard many stories of whole families helping children learn school assignments and letting their imagination run wild. That is an easy and fun way to learn. When people use the methods together they seem to encourage each other and accomplish much more than someone working on their own. Try the stunts with your brothers and sisters. Perform some stunts together and surprise your friends.

Chapter 12
Playing a memory party game

When I was a teenager we used to play a party game where we would sit in a circle and the first person would say, 'I went to the store and bought a spanner.' The next person would say, 'I went to the store and bought a spanner and a camera.' Each person had to repeat what had already been bought in the correct order and add one at the end. Anyone who missed an item or said them in the wrong order was out of the game. Each player would try to make his new item difficult for everyone else to remember. The winner was the one who lasted the longest without making any mistakes.

I went to the store and bought a spanner, a camera and a left-handed screwdriver. I went to the store and bought a spanner, a camera, a left-handed screwdriver and a rhubarb-flavoured ice cream with a cherry on top. Making the items complicated made it even harder and more fun—after a while someone was bound to buy a left-handed spanner, or they would say a camera with a cherry on top!

The game was fun. I thought it was fun because I always did well. I would have done even better if I had known the technique I am going to teach you in this chapter.

Often when I am teaching a private student I will give a list of 10 or more words and ask the student to call them back, in forward and reverse order. It is a good brain sharpener and is good practice for making mental connections.

Making links

I taught this method to a group of educational psychologists and counsellors close to where I lived. I saw one of the people from the group a week later and he was eager to tell me how he had put the skills he had learned to good use.

He was counselling a young boy with learning difficulties and he taught him how to link information to learn long lists. He gave the boy 10 or more items to learn and had him call them back backwards and forwards. He told the boy, 'You don't have a learning disability. You just haven't learned how to learn.'

As they were leaving the classroom, the bell rang and they were joined by other students in the corridor. The other students saw the boy with his helper and told him he was backward and needed help.

The counsellor said, 'James [not his name] isn't stupid. He is probably smarter than any of you.'

They jeered at this statement so the counsellor said, 'Okay, James. I am going to call out 12 words and I want you to call them back in the same order.'

He then called out the words James had just learned—James's face lit up. Then James called them out correctly, and then in reverse order.

The counsellor told me the other kids were astonished, and followed James down the corridor saying, 'James, how did you do that? That was brilliant.'

James had done something his classmates couldn't do. That was great for his self-esteem. This is a favourite exercise with my students.

The essential difference between the link system and the reminder system is that with the reminder system you join the word or object to be memorised with the reminder; with the link method you join each object with the next.

This is a fun exercise to practise making links with objects that have no normal connection with each other. It is a fun way to sharpen your mind and to improve your creative thinking skills.

Tip

With the link method you remember each item by joining each object to the next.

The linking list method

You are given a list of words to memorise. Let's say the words are pen, clock, book, water, cushion, fridge, magpie, piano, roof, rollerblades, horse, calculator.

- The first word in the list is *pen*. You would normally join the first word to the reason for learning the list. In this case you don't have a reason so you join it to yourself or to the person giving you the list. Picture drawing tattoos all over your face with your pen. See yourself looking in the mirror while you draw the tattoos with the pen. Make the pen extra big so you can hardly hold it. Can you *see* it?

- Now join pen to the next word in the list, *clock*. Picture a large clock that has pens for hands: a short pen for the hour hand and a long pen for the minute hand.

- The next word is *book*. It would be obvious to link book with pen but we have finished with pen. We have to join clock to book. I imagine a picture where my book has a built-in clock and it allows me to read for 30 minutes at a time, then the alarm goes and the book closes. Picture it.

- The next word is *water*. You could see yourself pouring water over your prized book and wrecking it, or maybe you are reading your book underwater.

- After water comes *cushion*. Picture the cushions on your lounge all filled with water and they spring a leak when you sit on them. You could use the cushions as water pistols and squirt your family.

- Next comes *fridge*. Picture filling your fridge with cushions from the lounge so that they will cool you down when you sit on them.

- The next word is *magpie*. I picture my fridge filled with magpies. They have chosen to live in your fridge because it is too hot outside. They talk to you (talking magpies) each time you open the fridge door.

- After magpie comes *piano*. I see magpies playing my piano and playing it well. See your family applauding the magpies as they play a concerto.

- Next comes *roof*. You have your piano on the roof and if you want to play it you have to climb onto the roof. See yourself playing the piano on the roof.

- Next comes *rollerblades*. See yourself rollerblading over your roof and doing sharp turns as you come to the gutter.

- Rollerblades has to remind us of *horse*. I picture a horse on rollerblades skating down your street. The horse is very fast and definitely talented.

- The last word is *calculator*. We join calculator to horse. Picture a horse using your calculator to find square roots and do long division.

Test yourself

Now close the book and call back the list of words. You joined the first word to yourself. What was it? And that reminds you of?

If you missed any words, go over the list again making more vivid pictures in your mind. Now call them back again. Did you get them all?

Now surprise yourself and call the list out backwards.

Calculator reminds you of? Call back all 12 words.

This is an amazing feat and also fun to do!

Example: The facts speak for themselves

I gave a list of 15 words to a young boy I was teaching and he called them back in the same order and then called the list out backwards.

His astounded mother said to me, 'Look at this.' She pulled a sheet of paper from her handbag and showed it to me. It was a report from a respected medical centre that reported that her son had been tested and was capable of remembering three words in sequence.

He had just called back 15 words in sequence.

(continued)

Example: The facts speak for themselves *(cont'd)*

I would make a couple of observations. First, don't take any report on a child's abilities as written in concrete. In fact, be cautious with any negative assessment. I have heard people say, 'I can't do that. I have been tested and they tell me that I am not capable of learning this or doing that.' The report has a negative, limiting effect.

Second, they will tell you that my test with the boy doesn't count because I taught him how to learn the words. I would reply that anyone who is able to memorise a long list of words in sequence has a system or a method for doing it. I would also tell the boy not to volunteer the information about how he did it. If the people doing the tests don't know he has a method, then the results are valid.

Using these methods to learn quickly and accurately will put you up in the top one per cent of the population. No wonder people can't believe you are actually doing it!

Play and experiment with your own lists.

Missing number stunt

Here is a stunt you can perform that will help you learn the reminders better and make good mental pictures as well as impress your friends.

Have your friends write down the numbers from one to 30 on a piece of paper. Tell them to circle any one of the numbers and not to call it out to you.

Now tell them to call out the other numbers in random order and cross them out as they go so they know which numbers have been called. Tell them to call them slowly because you are going to tell them the circled number, or the number that wasn't called out.

As they call each number, imagine damaging the reminder for that number. If they call one, picture running and falling and skinning your knee. If the number is eight, imagine someone smashing your gate with a sledgehammer. If the number is 12, see someone harming swans at the lake.

Then, when they have called out all the numbers (except the circled number, of course) you mentally run through the reminders until you reach the undamaged one. You will recognise it immediately. You will be surprised how easy it is, but you will amaze your friends.

I performed this stunt with my fellow students in my class at teachers college. They said I must have added each number as they called it and subtracted my total from a grand total. The problem was, they blundered and actually missed two numbers. I told them both the numbers they had missed. I said that if I had added the numbers like they said then I would have given the sum of the two numbers.

People can't believe what you are actually doing.

 Tip

Don't forget: when they call you genius, don't argue with them, just look modest, but don't tell them how you did it!

More stunts

And don't forget to challenge your friends to give you 20 words to memorise. Ask them to come up with concrete nouns—something tangible, that you could see and touch, like clock, bird, mirror, tree. Ask them not to give intangible words, such as success, happiness or love. Tangible nouns are easier to connect with your reminders so stick to them as much as possible.

Ask them to give the words in random order, such as, 13, car; 5, pen; 1, calendar; 20, lake; until they have called out all 20. I repeat my warning, don't be tempted to review the words and numbers already called—just be careful to make good mental pictures for each item. Then call them back as fast as you can say them. You will be surprised how easy this is. Then call them out backwards. Then ask for numbers and call out the object. Then have them call the object and you give the number. Your friends will be impressed and you are developing your abilities.

Key points

- You can make links between the words in a list in order to remember the list.

- See the image in your mind so you will remember it easily.

- Remember to make the object or the link big or weird— exaggerating the image makes it easier to remember.

- Keep the method to yourself and go on amazing friends and experts with your skills.

More activities to try

Try the following stunts and impress your friends.

⚙ Use the reminders to plan your day.

⚙ Use the reminders to remember page numbers in the books you read for fun.

⚙ Use the reminders to remember the numbers of players in the team you follow.

⚙ Try the missing number stunt described earlier in the chapter.

⚙ Try learning this list: CD, carpet, table, school, police, headphones, envelope, jacket, football, tree, bike, window.

⚙ Ask your family or friends to give you a list of words. Tell them they have to be things that you can touch like telephone or pen or book. Tell them you are just sharpening your brain. Then call them back, and then in reverse order.

⚙ Challenge your friends to call out the numbers one to 30 in jumbled order, leaving out one number. Damage each reminder as they call them out and you will be surprised how easy it is to recognise the number that hasn't been damaged.

Chapter 13
Learning word-for-word

There are many times when we want to learn something word-perfect. It might be a passage of Shakespeare, poetry, a definition, or a passage from the Bible or another holy book. You don't want to learn what the passage says in essence: you want to learn it perfectly, word for word.

Many people panic when they have to memorise something word-perfect. Certainly it seems like hard work, but that should be no reason to fear it. I am going to show you a simple method that will not only take the hard work out of learning; it will make word-for-word memorisation easy and fun.

I often throw out the challenge in seminars and classes: give me a passage you have to memorise and I will learn it with you. Students are amazed at how easy word-for-word memorisation can be.

At a seminar in Adelaide, South Australia, I gave the challenge: give me a quotation and I will have the entire audience memorise it without effort. One lady gave me a quotation from Shakespeare, others gave Bible quotations and quotations from famous men and women.

Let's see how we would memorise a small portion of the inauguration speech by President John F. Kennedy.

'Ask not what your country can do for you—ask what you can do for your country.'

The usual method for memorising a passage like this would be to say: 'Ask not what your country can do for you. Ask not what your country can do for you. Ask not what your country can do for you…' We would repeat this at least a dozen more times until we thought we could remember it.

Then we would say: 'Ask what you can do for your country. Ask what you can do for your country. Ask what you can do for your country…' and keep repeating it until we had learned it.

Then we would repeat, 'Ask not what your country can do for you—ask what you can do for your country. Ask not what your country can do for you—ask what you can do for your country.'

I think you get the idea. The method is mind numbing, but it is the only method we know. No wonder people hate the idea of word-for-word memorisation.

Here's my method

Here is how I, and everyone in the audience, memorised the quotation, much more quickly and easily.

Firstly, I underlined the important words. It looked like this.

<u>Ask not</u> what your <u>country</u> <u>can do for you</u>—<u>ask</u> what <u>you can do</u> for your <u>country</u>.

Then I numbered the underlined sections. 'Ask not' was 1, 'country' was 2 and so on.

   1   2   3   4

<u>Ask not</u> what your <u>country</u> <u>can do for you</u>—<u>ask</u> what

   5   6

<u>you can do</u> for your <u>country</u>.

Then we joined each underlined word or group of words to a reminder.

Let's memorise the quote

Here's how we can use the reminders to learn the quotation.

1 run   ask not

2 shoe   country

3 tree   can do for you

4 door   ask

5 hive   you can do

6 sticks   country.

Now we simply join the reminders—one, run—to the words to memorise the passage.

1 We join *run* with *ask not*. *Ask not* to join in our race. You are not allowed.

2 We join two, *shoe*, with *country*. I imagine going to a shoe store and saying you want strong shoes to wear in the country—you want *country shoes*.

3 Three, *tree, can do for you*. You go to a tree nursery to buy a tree and you ask, 'What can the *tree do for me*?'

4 Four, *door*, reminds us of *ask*. I simply picture someone is knocking on your door and you *ask*, 'Who's there?'

5 Five, *hive*, has to remind us of *you can do*. Someone asks you to remove a beehive from their porch. You say *you can do* it.

6 *Sticks* has to remind us of *country*. I imagine walking through the country using a large stick as a walking aid.

The connections aren't perfect, but they only have to work for one or two minutes until we make our first revision. First I call back the connections. Then I look at the words that fill the gaps and take note of the meaning of the quote. I also note how the words go. The quote begins, 'ask not', not 'don't ask'. It is a fairly simple quote which makes it more powerful and also easy to learn. That is the easy way to learn anything word-for-word.

Now we should be able to call back the whole passage from memory. Please do so.

If you didn't get it exactly right, you would have been very close. It won't take much effort now to learn it word-perfect.

This is much easier and much more fun than repeating the passage over and over and hoping it will stick by itself.

If someone fed you cues each time you forgot your lines, they would probably say just one or two words to remind you — that would be all you would need, and the reminder system works the same way.

I have had students memorise long passages from Shakespeare and the Bible, and many university students use this method to learn legislation and legal definitions and regulations. Sunday School teachers have told me it is an easy and fun way to teach their class to memorise Bible verses. This is by far the easiest method where word-for-word memorisation is necessary.

 Tip

If you don't want to learn the second verse of 'Advance Australia Fair', skip the next activity and try learning an extract from a famous speech by Winston Churchill, Britain's eloquent leader in the Second World War (it's given at the end of this chapter).

Let's learn the second verse of 'Advance Australia Fair'

Most Australians know the words of the first verse of the national anthem but most don't even know that a second verse exists. Actually there are a number of other verses to the song, but the following has been officially recognised as the second verse of the national anthem.

Let's use the reminder system to learn the words. We underline and then give a number to the important words and phrases.

    1   2   3

Beneath our radiant Southern Cross

      4   5

We'll toil with hearts and hands;

    6   7

To make this Commonwealth of ours

   8   9

Renowned of all the lands;

         10

For those who've come across the seas

    11   12

We've boundless plains to share;

    13   14

With courage let us all combine

To Advance Australia Fair.

In joyful strains then let us sing,

Advance Australia Fair.

I haven't numbered words in the final three lines because they are the same as the end of the first verse.

Now we have:

1	run	beneath
2	shoe	radiant
3	tree	Southern Cross
4	door	toil
5	hive	hearts and hands
6	sticks	make
7	heaven	Commonwealth
8	gate	renowned
9	dine	lands
10	hen	who've come across the seas
11	pencil	boundless
12	swan	share
13	McDonald's	courage
14	yacht	combine.

Let's join them to memorise the second verse with the minimum of effort.

How the reminders work for 'Advance Australia Fair'

1 I picture running beneath the water for number one.

2 Two, shoe, has to join with radiant. I picture running shoes with lights that shine when you walk. They are radiant.

3 Three, tree, joins with Southern Cross. I picture a Christmas tree with, instead of one star, I see the whole Southern Cross on the top.

4 Four, door, has to remind us of toil. I see a whole team of workers toiling to fix the door to my room.

5 Five, hive, joins with hearts and hands. Where do the bees sting us? On our hearts and our hands.

6 I use sticks to make a huge fort on the floor of my room. I make the fort one stick at a time.

7 Seven, heaven, reminds us of Commonwealth. I picture going up to heaven and being confronted by the whole commonwealth of angels. They ask me if I am willing to join.

8 Eight, gate, has to remind me of renowned. Berlin's Brandenburg Gate is renowned around the world. Imagine that you have a similar gate outside your house and it is renowned.

9 Lands has to join with dine for nine, so I picture going to restaurants around the world and eating exotic dishes from different lands.

10 Ten, hen, joins with who've come across the seas. I picture thousands of hens disembarking from huge ships as they arrive from across the seas.

11 The reminder for eleven is pencil because the numbers in the teens use the look-alike reminders. Eleven is boundless. The opportunities for using our pencil are boundless because there is no limit to what we can write. It is boundless.

12 Twelve is swan and reminds us of share. I picture feeding swans with crusts of bread and telling the swans they have to share. There is a greedy swan who wants it all for itself.

13 Thirteen is courage and the reminder is McDonald's. Someone comes in to McDonald's wearing a balaclava and holds them up. He wants to steal their hamburgers. The workers show great courage in bringing the vicious crook to the ground until the police arrive.

14 Fourteen is combine and the reminder is yacht or sailboat. I picture the crews of two yachts combine to combine their two yachts into a catamaran. So, the yachts have combined and the crews have combined. How can we forget that 14 is combine?

Now read the words of the second verse through again and see the pictures as you do so. Take notice of the words that join the words you memorised.

Test yourself

Now call back the whole verse from memory.

Even if you made a couple of mistakes, this is still the easiest and the most enjoyable way to learn the verse word-for-word.

Key points

- Underline the key words in the quotation and learn them using the reminder system.

- The reminder method takes the drudgery out of learning word-for-word.

- With the reminder method there is no rote learning or endless repetition.

 More activities to try

- Do you have any favourite poems or songs you would like to learn? Learn them using this easy method and you will learn them in half the time with half the effort.

- Memorise this quote from a speech by Winston Churchill:

  Never give in. Never give in. Never, never, never, never — in nothing, great or small, large or petty — never give in, except to convictions of honour and good sense. Never yield to force. Never yield to the apparently overwhelming might of the enemy.

Chapter 14
Memorising big numbers

A number of students, both boys and girls, tell me that they want to memorise the value of pi to 50 or 100 decimal places, purely to show off. (The value of pi is how much you multiply the distance across a circle—diameter—to get the distance around it—the circumference. It is about 3.14159, but there are an infinite number of digits in the value.) One boy told me that they had the value of pi to 150 decimal places around the mathematics room at his school. He asked his friends to put the classroom rubbish bin over his head and he recited the 150 numbers of pi without being able to see it. Then he told them to call out four or five digits together from anywhere in the number and he would continue calling them. Then he recited the number backwards. His friends couldn't believe it.

He got a reputation for being a genius. He remembered my advice never to argue with anyone who calls you a genius.

Remembering numbers

Numbers rules our lives. We have to remember our street numbers, telephone numbers, PINs, account numbers, room numbers, and then in class we have to know the value of pi, populations, latitudes and longitudes, distances and dates—there seems to be no end to the numbers we need to carry in our heads.

Most people find it difficult to remember numbers. It doesn't matter what subjects you are studying, you will find that numbers are involved. History is full of dates to learn, populations and the size of armies; geography has distances and populations; science is full of numbers; even art and music have their own numbers and dates to learn.

We could use logical reminders for hundreds digits, use look-alikes for 10s and rhyming for units—but there's an easier way. In this chapter I am going to show you an easy way to learn big numbers so you will never forget them.

Phonetic values

What is easier to remember, a six-digit number or a single word? You are about to learn a method where you can change numbers into words. There are just 10 simple values to learn, and even then no rote memory is involved.

Ernest E. Wood, in his book, *Mind and Memory Training* (Theosophical Publishing House, 1936), tells how, when he was recuperating from a long illness in around 1910, he looked at systems for memorising numbers and found them to be deficient—they were too complicated. So he devised his own system, which has been adopted by mathematicians and memory experts around the world. This is something that every student should learn. Here is how it works.

Each digit has a phonetic value so that words can be converted to numbers, and numbers to words.

1 = t   the letter 't' has one downstroke, or it looks like a number one with a short horizontal crossbar.

2 = n   the letter 'n' has two downstrokes.

3 = m   the letter 'm' has three downstrokes. Also, if you put the letter 'm' on its side it looks like a 3.

4 = r   the letter 'r' is the fourth letter of the word 'four'.

5 = L   if you hold out your left hand in front of you with the palm facing away, and your fingers together and your thumb out, your hand forms the capital letter L. Remember, 5 fingers = L. Also, L in Roman numerals equals 50.

At this stage, keeping your place, close the book and repeat the phonetic values of the numbers one to five.

Easy, wasn't it? You learnt them without realising that you were committing them to memory.

Let's continue with the rest of the phonetic reminders. (Table 14.1 shows illustrated examples of the reminders.)

6 = J   the letter J looks like the mirror image of 6, or a 6 back to front.

7 = K   the letter K can be written by using two sevens, one seven upright and one upside down.

8 = F   a handwritten F has two loops like an eight.

9 = P   P is a mirror image of the number 9.

0 = Z   Z is the initial letter of the word 'zero'.

Table 14.1: the reminders for the numbers from six to zero, showing illustrated examples

Phonetic reminder	Clue	Number	Illustration
6 = J	The letter J looks like the mirror image of 6, or a 6 back to front	6	
7 = K	The letter K can be written by using two sevens, one seven upright and one upside down.	7	

(continued)

Table 14.1: the reminders for the numbers from six to zero, showing illustrated examples *(cont'd)*

Phonetic reminder	Clue	Number	Illustration
8 = F	A handwritten letter F has two loops like an eight.	8	
9 = P	The letter P is a mirror image of the number 9.	9	
0 = Z	Z is the initial letter of the word 'zero'.	0	

Test yourself

Now close the book again and call off the phonetic values of one to zero from memory. If you make a mistake, read the explanation for that digit again and try them through once more. No doubt you got them all right on the second attempt.

Turning the letters into words

You will notice that the phonetic equivalents of the digits are all consonants. The vowels, a, e, i, o, u, have no phonetic value in this system. Therefore, to make a word equal the number 12, you would take the equivalent of 1 (=t) and 2 (=n), and by inserting a vowel between, you can form the words tan, ten, tin, ton, teen, tone and tune. You can choose the word you want to use as your reminder for the number you are learning.

Example: Let's look at some numbers

Take a pencil and paper and see how many words you can form with the value of 91.

By taking the value of 9 and the value of 1 and inserting vowels, you should be able to come up with quite a few. Don't read any further without making the attempt, even if you try without writing them down.

What is the value of 9? Remember the mirror image? And the value of 1? Again remember, one downstroke. Your list might look something like this: pat, pet, pit, pot, put, pate, peat, poet. Are you getting the idea now?

Let's look at it from the other direction. What is the phonetic value of the word 'moon'? How about the word 'man'? You should have said 32 for both words: m = 3, n = 2.

What is the value of these words: tire, tar and tree?

Did you say 14?

A few simple rules

Now let's look at a few simple rules. We call these phonetic values because we give each consonant a value according to how it is pronounced.

- A silent letter has no value, such as the K in knife, knob and knee; the B in comb, lamb and limb; and the L in palm and walk. This also means that if a C is pronounced like a K, as in carry or can, it has a value of 7, the same as K.

- Say the letters T and D out loud! Did you notice that you position your tongue the same way to make both sounds? A T is like a hard D, so in our system they both have a value of one.

- Say the words out loud, 'Kay' and 'Gay'. Did you notice that these sounds are similar, with the K and hard G pronounced at the back of the throat? Both K and hard G have a value of seven.

- V and F are both pronounced with your upper teeth on your lower lip. An F is a hard V. They both have a value of eight. 'Ph' in photo is pronounced like an F and has the same value, eight.

- B and P are both formed with the lips (try it!) and have the same value, nine. Thinking of BP (British Petroleum) will help you remember this.

- The J sound for six is similar to many sounds in English: soft G in magic. (Jeff and Geoff are pronounced the same way.) The letters 'dge' in 'edge' equal six; 'sh' in shoe and 'ch' in chew also have a value of six. S in treasure and C in ocean are also six.

- You will readily see that Z and S have a similar sound. They both equal zero. A soft C, as in 'cent' is pronounced the same as an S (sent, cent) and has the value of zero as well.

- The only consonants without value are W, H and Y, and these are easily remembered because they spell the word, 'why'. Table 14.2 shows the phonetic values.

Table 14.2: pronunciation determines the value of any letter

Number	Phonetic value (sounds)	Reminder (looks like)
1	t, d	t has one downstroke.
2	n	n has two downstrokes.
3	m	m has three downstrokes.
4	r	r is the fourth letter of the word 'four'. For our purposes, R is always pronounced.
5	L	L = 50 in Roman numerals. The left hand with fingers together and thumb out makes an 'L' with five fingers (including thumb).
6	J, sh, ch, tch, soft G, dge	r is the fourth letter of the word 'four'.
7	K, hard C, hard G	K can be written with two sevens.
8	F, V, ph	Handwritten F looks like an eight.
9	P, B	P looks like a back-to-front 9.
0	Z, S	Zero begins with Z.

Vowels have no value.

Silent letters have no value.

The consonants W, H, Y (why) have no value.

Double letters that don't change the consonant sound have the value of a single letter.

Double letters, such as double T in butter or double B in rabbit, are pronounced the same way as if they were single letters. Therefore, 'matter' would have a value of 314, not 3114. 'Letter' would be 514, not 5114. Be careful though with words like 'accent' where each C is pronounced differently; the first C is 7 (pronounced like K) and the second is zero (pronounced like S.)

Using the phonetic values to memorise numbers

How would you memorise the number 415? The numbers have the sounds RTL. That could be made into rattle, riddle or retail. Readily would also have a value of 415 but would be hard to picture.

How about 125? Tunnel, Daniel and tonal each have a value of 125. It is a matter of trying different vowels to see which words you can make.

How would you remember the value of pi? Pi has a value of 3.141592653579. The value rounded off to eight digits to fill an eight-digit calculator would be 3.1415927. An easy way to remember the number is to convert it to ma turtle bank.

Ask yourself, who is baking the pie? Ma. What kind of pie is it? A turtle pie. Where do you go to get it? A turtle bank.

Picture this: Ma goes to a turtle bank and says, 'I want to withdraw two turtles. I want to bake a turtle pie.' The letters are Ma TuRTLe BaNK
      3 1   4 15 9 2 7

You will never forget the value of pi.

Memorise your PIN

I use this method to memorise the PINs (personal identification numbers) for credit cards and telephone accounts. Let's say I had a PIN of 8435, which converts to FoRMaL. I picture having to dress formally each time I have to visit my bank or they wouldn't let me through the door. Make a picture that joins the number to the particular card or establishment.

Going to the library

I told my wife I was going to the library. She asked me if I could borrow some books on gardening for her. I said I could, but what was the Dewey decimal number for gardening? (All reference books are catalogued under a number. For instance, language books are catalogued in the 400s, science in the 500s.)

Barb said she didn't know, but got a book she had already borrowed and said, 'The number is 635.'

I tried the phonetic equivalents, JML. I tried jammel, jemmel, jimmel, jommel, jummel. None of them worked so I tried the long vowels, jamel, jemel, jimel, jomel, jumel. No help there either so I changed the J to sh. Shammel, shemmel, shimmel... I stopped there. Wayne Schimmelbusch was captain of the North Melbourne football team. The first part of his name, Schimmel, gave the Dewey number, 635, and the second part, busch, gave the category. It is not often you get such a beautiful match, but I treasure them when I find them.

More things to remember

You can use this system to memorise all of your friend's telephone numbers. Dates, prices, specifications, quantities, in fact, anything to do with numbers becomes easy to memorise using this system.

Columbus discovered America in 1492. Children memorise the date by the rhyme, 'In fourteen hundred and ninety-two, Columbus sailed the ocean blue.' The problem with this is that it would work for fifteen hundred and ninety-two just as well. We can use the phonetic values to remember the date accurately. We know that Columbus discovered America in the last millennium so we only need to memorise the last three digits, and then 492 gives us robin. What were the sailors afraid of when they sailed with Columbus? Falling off the end of the world! I think of the story of Noah on the ark sending out a dove to see if the flood had receded and if there was land above the water. I picture Columbus sending out a robin and it returns with a feather from an American Indian's war bonnet. Robin gives me 492 so I remember it happened in 1492.

Please read through this section again to make sure you have learned all the phonetic values.

Now test yourself

Here is a test to see how well you have mastered the material in this section. What are the phonetic values of the following words?

- roof
- bat
- light
- paint
- tent
- vision
- comb
- computer

Cover the answers below and call out the numbers. Check your answers one at a time.

The answers are:

- roof   48
- bat   91
- light   51
- paint   921
- tent   121
- vision   862
- comb   73
- computer   73914

Did you get them all right? Make sure of the rules for the values you got wrong and try them again. This time you should get them all correct.

Practise changing numbers to words and words to numbers until it becomes automatic. This is how I memorise telephone numbers. I have changed my bank ID numbers to words so I type the numbers while I say the words.

Remember that R is always pronounced in this system. In some parts of England, New Zealand and Australia, we tend to pronounce many words as if the R wasn't there. For instance, the words form, farm, arm, turn — and even word — are pronounced as if the 'r' were missing.

'Th' has the value of one, but we will avoid using it where we can.

The letters 'ng' have a value of 27. Sing equals 027 and long equals 527.

Phonetic reminders

You can use the phonetic value system to make more reminders. You can extend this list as far as you like.

Here is a list of my phonetic reminders, which I use every day. You can use these or change any you don't like.

1 Tie

2 Noah

3 Ma

4 Rye

5 Law

6 Shoe

7 Cow

8 Ivy

9 Bee

10 Toes.

Each reminder has the phonetic value of the number it represents.

1 'Tie' is 1 because it has a value of one. I use a necktie.

2 The number 2 is Noah, the gentleman who built the ark to save himself and the animals in the flood. Noah has a phonetic value of 2.

3   The number 3 is ma—your mother or someone who represents mother to you.

4   The number 4 is rye, meaning rye bread. I use any loaf of bread for four.

5   The number 5 is law. I link what I am learning with the police.

6   Number 6 is shoe. Because shoe is number two in my rhyming reminder list I am careful that I don't mix lists. I either change 6 to jaw or watch or 2 shoe to 2 glue.

7   The number 7 is cow. Number 7 always uses the 4-legged kind of cow. Always stick to the same meaning or cow won't remind you of anything.

8   The number 8 is ivy, the stuff that grows over old buildings.

9   The number 9 is bee—always an attacking bee. If you combine this list with the rhyming reminders, use drive for five.

10   And 10 is toes. The word toes has a phonetic value of 10 (t = 1 and s = 0) and you probably have 10 of them.

There should be no rote memory involved in learning those reminders because the numbers themselves give the clue. All of the reminders begin with the phonetic value except for eight, ivy.

Test yourself

What words can you find to equal the following numbers?

- 86
- 72
- 743
- 941
- 215
- 701.

Here are some possibilities for remembering those numbers:

- 86   fish, fetch, fiche
- 72   coin, gun, can, gain, cane, goon, cone
- 743   cream, crumb, cram, grim, grime, groom, gram, crime, chrome
- 941   bread, brat, bright, brought, breed, bride, bored
- 215   needle, nettle
- 701   cassette, cast, gust, guest, kissed, cased, cost.

It doesn't take much effort to learn these values and the return is well worth it. It is easy now to memorise any numbers you will need to know for your tests and exams, as well as everyday numbers such as your bank PIN or your student number.

Key points

- Phonetic values are not learnt by rote.

- Vowels have no value.

- One letter can have more than one value — it depends on the pronunciation.

- You can use several words for longer numbers.

- Phonetic reminders add to the number of reminder lists you can use.

- Phonetic values make it easy to memorise longer numbers.

More activities to try

- When you are out either in a car or walking, practise changing the car number plates that you see into words. You will have to make words for three-digit numbers.

- Here is the value of pi to 30 decimal places. Change the numbers to words and link them 3.1415926535 8979323846 2643383279.

- Memorise the telephone numbers of your friends.

- How many postcodes can you memorise?

Chapter 15
Learning the US presidents

Often we have to learn information that cannot be pictured. How do you picture names of viruses, cities you know nothing about, or people's names? There are many things we have to learn that simply cannot be pictured in our minds as something tangible. That is when we have to ask ourselves, what sounds like the word I have to remember?

I used to think I had no natural ability in this area. I found it difficult to make puns or to make a 'play on words'. With practice I found it came a little more easily, but I still found it difficult. I was asked to give classes teaching students how to learn difficult lists and I had to find sound-alikes. I didn't like it and I still found it hard to do, but I was desperate and found I could find them, often at the last moment. Then people began to tell me I must have a natural talent for it.

It is much easier if you look for sound-alikes with a friend or as part of a group.

I discovered that a natural talent for most things comes with a lot of practice and hard work. But, here is the good news. The method works even if you can't get it to work. What do I mean? If you can't think of any word that sounds like the word you need to remember you are still concentrating on the word, trying to think of a word or words that sound like the one you need to remember. That concentration is far greater than the passive learning or rote learning you would normally do so you are still more likely to remember it.

Or, what if you can't make a good association, or picture connection in your mind? Trying to make the connection will probably work for you in the short term. Then, with your first or second review, make a good association. So the method will work for you even if it doesn't come easily.

Tip

If you use your imagination, you can make the learning fun for any material or subject. It is up to you.

The general rule for learning abstract information when you don't know what it looks like or it is too vague to picture, is to look for a word that *sounds* like the word you are trying to learn or look for something to represent the quality or the meaning.

And remember, using your own sound-alikes and pictures will work better than the ones you have been given. Making your own pictures will force a much higher level of concentration, and make learning easier.

Remembering the names of US presidents

Let's try this idea of remembering abstract information by memorising a list of the first 20 US presidents. Here's the list we are going to remember:

1 Washington

2 Adams

3 Jefferson

4 Madison

5 Monroe

6 Adams

7 Jackson

8 Van Buren

9 Harrison

10 Tyler

11 Polk

12 Taylor

13 Fillmore

14 Pierce

15 Buchanan

16 Lincoln

17 Johnson

18 Grant

19 Hayes

20 Garfield.

Presidents 1 to 10

We use the rhyming reminders and sound-alikes to learn presidents 1 to 10.

1 The first president of the United States was George Washington. How do you remember that? You could think of Washington DC or the state of Washington in the United States. To use the method for remembering abstract words I would use a sound-alike. Washing machine sounds enough like Washington to enable me to remember it. I picture my washing machine is running away from home and my whole family is chasing it down your street to bring it back. Decide on a picture and *see* it.

2 Two, shoe, reminds us of the second president, John Adams. For Adams you could think of Adam, the first man, a dam, or an atom bomb. (Atom sounds like Adams.) I see myself wearing atom bombs strapped to my feet instead of shoes.

3 Three, tree, was President Jefferson. Picture the tree in your yard asking another tree with a little tree growing below it, 'D'y'ave a son?' (Dj'ave a son = Did you have a son = Jefferson.) It is corny, but it will work and that's all that matters.

4 Four, door, was President Madison. Madison sounds like medicine. I picture the door to the medicine cupboard with a huge lock on it so toddlers can't open it.

5 Five, hive, is President Monroe. You could use Marilyn Monroe or 'man row' as in a man rowing a boat. See a man rowing a boat as fast as he can because a swarm of bees is chasing him. See it.

You have now learnt the first five presidents of the United States!

6 Six, sticks, is President John Quincy Adams. I use atom bomb again. Someone explodes an atom bomb

and all of the city just becomes a pile of sticks. Everything is blown up. That will do it.

7 Seven, heaven, was President Andrew Jackson. What does Jackson sound like? You could have jack son—jack being a car jack. I picture using a car jack to lift myself into heaven. Or your father is jacking you up into heaven—that gives you Jackson.

8 Eight, gate, was President Van Buren. I think of the Federal *Bureau* (of Investigation—the FBI) using a surveillance *van*, and it is parked by your gate to keep an eye on you.

9 Nine, dine, was President Harrison. You are eating your meal and your friend wants to play or you are running late for school so your parents keep saying, 'Hurry son'.

10 Ten, hen, is President Tyler. Tyler sounds exactly like tiler, someone who lays tiles. I picture a hen laying tiles in your bathroom.

Now, hold your place in the book and call out the first 10 presidents of America from memory. Wasn't that the easiest way to learn the presidents?

Wasn't that much easier and more enjoyable than memorising them by rote? Can you see that you can enjoy yourself even learning subjects you aren't very interested in? But, if you like the subject, this method removes most of the effort and stress.

You can have fun learning the names of the next presidents.

Presidents 11 to 20

We now use the look-alike reminders and sound-alikes for presidents 11 to 20.

11 Our reminder for 11 is pencil, the look-alike for one. The 11th president was President Polk. I picture someone *poking* a *pencil* in your eye. That will remind me the eleventh president was Polk.

12 The reminder for 12 is swan. The 12th president was President Taylor. A *tailor* makes clothes so I picture a *swan* wearing a three-piece suit and looking very smart. See it.

13 The 13th president was President Fillmore. I imagine the local *McDonald's* has a new manager and he is telling the workers, 'You have to *fill more* burgers.' You won't forget President Fillmore.

14 Number 14, yacht, was President Pierce. What happens if you pierce a sailboat? It sinks. Picture *piercing* a *sailboat* or a *yacht* and sinking it.

15 Number 15, nose, is President Buchanan. It sounds like blue cannon. This reminder is a bit gross, but I guarantee it will work. Imagine using your *nose* as a *cannon*. That will enable you to remember that Buchanan was the 15th president.

Now call back the presidents from one to 15.

16 Number 16 is yoyo and reminds us of President Lincoln. Lincoln sounds like *link on*. I picture making a link on the end of your yoyo string so you can fix it like a noose on your finger and it stays tight.

17 Number 17, boomerang, reminds us of President Johnson. See a long queue of boomerangs waiting to use the *john*.

18 Number 18, mask, reminds us of President Grant. Grant sounds enough like granite to remind me of his name. I see a criminal in a *face mask* throwing a

huge block of *granite* through the store window and making off with the jewellery.

19 Number 19 is tape measure and reminds me of President Hayes. I simply picture measuring *hay* in the field after the harvest and seeing if it measures up.

20 The 20th president was President Garfield. Garfield sounds like *car field*. Twenty is bat and ball, so we join bat and ball to car field. I picture hitting the ball out of the stadium and it causes damage in the car park with a lot of dents and broken windscreens.

Now close the book and call out all 20 presidents.

Wasn't that easy? If you missed one you simply make the picture again, adding more detail, and you have learnt them all. You call them straight back to ensure you have learnt them and then review them from time to time to put the list in your permanent memory. That is what I would call an excellent return for your effort.

Key points

- Look for a sound-alike word if the word you are learning is abstract or hard to visualise.

- If you can't find a sound-alike, find something to represent the word you are learning.

- You will get better with practice.

- Using your imagination can make learning subjects you don't like into fun.

- Try working out reminders with friends — it's fun and it works!

More activities to try

☼ Try making sound-alikes for the names of all the students in your class.

☼ Memorise the students in your class in alphabetical order. (That is, the same order of the roll call by giving them numbers.)

☼ Memorise the US presidents from 21 to 30 using the logical reminders. Here is the list:

21   Arthur

22   Cleveland

23   Harrison

24   Cleveland (2nd term)

25   McKinley

26   Roosevelt (Theodore)

27   Taft

28   Wilson

29   Harding

30   Coolidge.

 # Afterword

Congratulations on reaching the end of this book! You have learned a strategy for thinking and learning that will change your life if you use it.

Begin using the reminders immediately

Don't wait until you have mastered everything in the book perfectly to begin using what you have learned. Take out your textbooks and start learning now. Using the reminders will help you remember the reminders. That is the best way to learn them.

Try these stunts and impress your friends

Use the reminders to plan your day, to remember page numbers in the books you read for fun or to remember the numbers of players in your team you follow, for instance.

Perform the party stunts in chapter 12. Try them on a close family member first to assure yourself you can do it. That way, you won't be too embarrassed if you get it wrong.

Tip

Don't forget, when your friends call you a genius, just look modest, and don't tell them how you did it!

The methods work, but you won't benefit unless you use them

Yes, the methods do work. You have been using them and they have worked for you. Now put them to use with your studies and your life. Maybe you could even tackle some extra subjects or activities. I hope this book has raised your expectations.

I'd love to hear how you go. Please don't send me feedback that says, 'The methods were great, they worked for me. I am amazed at what I can do, but I haven't done anything with them since reading the book.' The methods will be of no benefit to you unless you use them.

I urge you to make the commitment now that you will use what you have learned so you will change and enrich your life. Then email me the result.

Bill Handley
Melbourne, Australia
bhandley@speedmathematics.com
www.speedmathematics.com

Frequently asked questions

Isn't memorising schoolwork just learning by rote — and isn't learning by rote a bad thing?

You are not learning by rote if you use the methods taught in this book. In fact we eliminate rote learning. Learning by rote involves repeating what you are learning over and over again. Most people regard rote learning as drudgery. My reminders method forces you to analyse what you are learning, and then summarise it. This is what high-achieving students do. They break down the information in their textbook to a few pages in their notebook and do their revision from their own notes. These methods result in a higher level of concentration and understanding of the material than achieved by traditional learning methods.

Normally, the only way to learn the words of a song or poetry is by rote; my method is much more efficient and much more pleasant.

Isn't understanding more important than parroting information?

I don't see this as a contest. Both understanding and remembering what you have learned are important. Why not do both? Actually, my methods will help your understanding of the material, because you need to analyse and summarise it to make your mental connections.

Isn't your method just a trick?

No, it is not a trick. To me, a trick implies trickery—that you aren't really doing what you appear to be doing. You *appear* to be learning the material and that is exactly what you *are* doing. You are just using a more efficient method than most people. If you can recall the information when you need it, you have really learned it.

How long will I remember what I have learned?

That is up to you. You decide whether to put the information you have learned into your long-term memory or whether you just want to remember the information for a specific purpose. If it is a list of things to pick up from the supermarket this afternoon, then you only need to retain it for an hour or so. If you want to keep the information in your long-term memory, then you need to review it every day for a week, then once a week for a month, and then occasionally from time to time to make sure the information is there when you need it.

Isn't the method just a crutch?

Certainly the method will enable you to learn and memorise information more easily. The question implies that there is something wrong with using a crutch. You only need the crutch until the information goes into your permanent long-term memory. Then you can discard the crutch because it has served its purpose. But, if you get stuck later and have difficulty recalling the information under pressure, you will be pleased you have a crutch to enable you to bring the information to mind when you need it.

Now I have twice as much to learn — the method plus the information I am studying. Aren't you just adding to my workload?

This question is almost always asked by people who haven't tried the method. First, the reminders only have to be learned once. They can then be used again and again. Second, the reminders are easily learned. There should be no rote memory involved. So, the double effort of learning the reminders plus the material to be studied becomes easier than learning the material by itself without any strategy.

My course doesn't just consist of learning facts. How will this help me?

First, the method forces you to analyse and summarise the material you are learning. The method also enables you to take effective notes. And it enables you to commit your ideas, arguments and interpretations of your subject to memory for instant recall. It is true that the methods are more easily applied to some subjects rather than to others, but they can still be applied in some way to any subject.

Why don't the methods work for me?

I have had students tell me that the methods aren't working for them. They'll say, 'I read through 30 names of presidents but I could only remember 26' or 'My friends gave me a list of 20 words to memorise and I could only call back 18. What's wrong?'

I ask them, when you read through the 30 presidents and could only call back 26, how many more did you have to learn? They'll say, 'Oh yes, I learned the other four the second time I read them through.'

When I say, 'So, you read the list through twice to learn all 30 names? How many times would you have to practise reading them to learn them before you learned these methods?' the reply is usually something like, 'Well, it would have taken me days to learn them.' And my reply is, 'So, your failures now are better than your greatest successes previously.'

When I have issued the challenge to give me 20 words in any order and I memorise them as you call them, I usually get them all but, occasionally I will miss one, or even two. I don't panic. I see the reminders for the numbers I missed and I ask myself, where was the reminder, what was it doing, what happened to it? I see the reminder as clearly as I can in my mind. If that doesn't work, I simply apologise and ask them for the word I missed. Then I say, to make up for my lapse I will call the list backwards and I say them as fast as I can. People usually say in response to this, 'He only pretended to forget the words.'

I have so much to learn, and the material is so complicated, how can the methods help me?

This question is often asked by medical and law students. They tell me they have so much to learn already. That is precisely why they need an effective method of study. If you didn't have much to learn you wouldn't need this book. The greater the amount to be learned, the more you need an effective method to do it. Learn the methods while you are young and you will have a huge advantage over your classmates.

Don't the methods give me an unfair advantage over everyone else?

All high-achieving students use better study methods than the students who don't do as well. They obviously have an advantage over students who have poor study methods. No one says that they have an unfair advantage or that they should be made to use poor study methods as well. If there is an easy way to learn and a difficult way, why use the difficult, ineffective methods?

Is it cheating to use the methods?

I have had students tell me that the methods are as good as cheating. They are speaking tongue in cheek. You are doing nothing dishonest by using good study methods. But some students have worried that it somehow gives them an unfair advantage. The methods you use will make absolutely no difference to how the other students perform. If you are worried you have an unfair advantage, teach the under-achieving students the methods yourself. There is no reason why everyone shouldn't succeed using this method.

I find it hard to make good mental pictures — what can I do to get better?

It's actually good if you find it hard to create mental pictures because the more difficulty you have determining a good picture or a sound-alike, the more you have to concentrate. That means you are even more likely to remember what you are learning.

Let's take an extreme case of learning the vocabulary of a foreign language. The foreign word doesn't sound like anything that makes any sense to you. You simply can't think of anything that sounds remotely the same. You sweat on it for five minutes before you give it up as a bad job. You have just spent five minutes concentrating on the foreign word, how it sounds and its meaning. You have probably learned it by the concentration alone.

That is why I tell people that the method works even when it doesn't.

I can't visualise. I just can't make pictures in my head — how can I use the system?

It doesn't matter — the method will still work for you. Simply try to make the mental picture and the effort will lock the information in your mind.

I wondered about this problem when I was in teachers college. I took on a class assignment to teach children at the school for the blind. I taught these methods and found they worked equally well with children who were born blind and children who lost their sight later in life. They all made some kind of mental picture. The children who were born blind made pictures involving their other senses. They could hear, feel and sense the events in the picture and they worked just as well. So, if you can't see the picture, use your other senses to make the connection.

Even if you can't do that, the effort of trying to make the mental picture will force high concentration so you will still be able to recall the information.

I have discovered that many of my students who have this problem develop the ability to visualise and so improve their mental performance.

How long will I need to use the reminders?

You will use them for as long as you need them. That might not sound like an answer, but it is true.

If you are using the information every day, you will find it will quickly go into your long-term memory and you won't need the reminder to recall it. But, if you are stuck or under pressure and your mind goes blank, the reminder gives you a method to retrieve the information. If you only use the information occasionally, then you will need to use the reminders to retrieve it when you need it.

I still use the reminders to remember information I learned 20 years ago. I am glad I made the reminders and the connections—I would have no way to remember it otherwise.

Isn't the method artificial?

I have told the story of the mother who came to see me with her young son. I gave him 15 words to memorise. He called them back in the correct order and then he was able to easily call them back in reverse order. He had linked the words to memorise them.

His mother showed me the report from the medical centre which stated her son had been tested as being able to recall a maximum of three words in succession. His mother had brought him to me to see if we could improve on his results. We did. The boy was intelligent and easily learned and applied the methods.

I reported this to educators and child psychologists, and they told me the results were invalid because I had coached the boy how to do well. The results didn't count. I now tell my students, don't volunteer any information to anyone who is testing you as to how you were able to learn the material. Then the results *will* count.

If you are actually doing what you appear to be doing then the results are valid. And, any mental exercise requires a method. There is something wrong when someone says that their method is valid but yours is not.

Index

More secrets of learning from Bill Handley

Wrightbooks

Teach Your Children Tables/
Speed Maths For Kids
special bindup edition

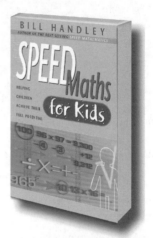

Speed Maths For Kids

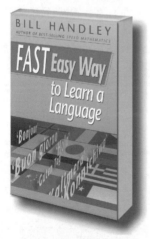

Fast, Easy Way to Learn
a Language

Speed Mathematics,
3rd edition

Available in print and e-book formats